THE
HEART
OF THE
PSALMS

The Heart of the Psalms
God's Word to the World

The Heart of the Psalms

978-1-7910-4056-7

978-1-7910-4057-4 eBook

The Heart of the Psalms: DVD

978-1-7910-4060-4

The Heart of the Psalms: Leader Guide

978-1-7910-4058-1

978-1-7910-4059-8 eBook

Cover description for *The Heart of the Psalms: God's Word to the World* by James C. Howell. The title is centered in white and gold text on a textured orange-red background framed in gold and white. Behind the title panel is Vincent van Gogh's painting *The Starry Night* (1889, oil on canvas). It features a swirling blue and yellow night sky, cypress trees, and a small village with a church steeple.

James C. Howell

— THE —

HEART
OF THE
PSALMS

GOD'S WORD TO
THE WORLD

Abingdon Press | Nashville

The Heart of the Psalms
God's Word to the World

Library of Congress Control Number: 2025939706
978-1-7910-4056-7

MANUFACTURED IN THE UNITED STATES OF AMERICA

In memory of
Thaniel Armistead and
Father Roland Murphy

Contents

Acknowledgments

A book like this happens only because of a host of people over many years: authors I've read, some of whom I've known personally; fellow students; other preachers; people sitting in classes I've taught; the A+ church members who find their way to my office to explore Scripture with me one on one; families in intensive care waiting rooms; and family members who've heard me read psalms.

Special thanks to Jason Byassee, Lynsley Smith, Wes Vander Lugt, Rob Lee, Meg Seitz, and my wife, Lisa, for reading and commenting. And what a privilege it has been to work with editors like James Rogers and Maria Mayo! It's a commonplace to thank others and declare that any remaining dumb stuff is mine. Who else is there to blame?

I've meant to write far more extensively on the Psalms than I've managed over these years since my doctoral work. With immense fondness and gratitude, and still some lingering grief, I dedicate this in memory of my friend and fellow seminarian Thaniel Armistead, with whom I read psalms daily in her hospital room, and who died before we could graduate together; and Father Roland Murphy, brilliant Psalms scholar, my teacher, doctoral adviser, mentor, and father figure. I never read any psalm without thinking of him.

Introduction

I love the Psalms. There's nothing special about me. Christians through the centuries have loved, prayed, chanted, sung, memorized, been puzzled by, and been enthralled with the Psalms. My love affair with the Psalms began not before or during seminary, but just after, as I'd embarked upon doctoral studies at Duke in Old Testament. I'd not intended to focus on the Psalms. The magnificent sagas of Genesis, the ribald narratives of David, or the biting critiques of the Prophets were more to my taste for research and publication—or so I thought.

As my studies progressed, my mentor and lead doctoral professor, Father Roland Murphy, helped me pick up extra cash by hiring me as his teaching assistant for several courses. I'd give a substitute lecture now and then, grade papers, and guide struggling students. A great experience for me! One day he called me into his office and roared (yes, he roared a bit like a lion when he spoke!) that he would be teaching the Psalms in the fall. Could I again be his assistant? Of course! I asked him how I should prepare. His norm was to rifle through his mountain of stacked and shelved books, retrieve nine or ten thick ones, most in German, slam them onto my lap and say, "Master these."

But this time, he eyed me—as if sizing up something not in my intellect but deep in my soul—and said, "Read one psalm in the morning and another in the evening—or rather, pray one and then another. By semester's beginning, you'll have waded through them all." I thought, *Wow, easy street. I got off light!*

Sauntering down the hallway toward home, I made my way across one quadrangle and entered the back of Duke Medical Center. A very dear friend and seminary classmate named Thaniel, twenty-three years old, was back in, suffering terribly from cystic fibrosis. After I found her room, I learned that her situation was growing more dire, and so she made a special request. Knowing the medical center was on my way from my apartment to the divinity school, she wondered if it would be too much trouble if I came by her room on my way in each morning and on my way home at day's end. Of course. I'd be honored to do so.

And then she asked, "When you stop by, could you read a psalm, one in the morning, another in the evening?"

Staggered, I recovered by asking, "Hey, you've been talking with Father Murphy, right?" She clearly had no idea what I was talking about.

And so I learned the Psalms, one by one, morning and evening, reading and praying them in a hospital room with a beloved young woman hanging on to life and on a path, inevitably, toward her death. Since that time, during some of my own dark nights of the soul, I have hung on to a psalm or two, or sometimes just a verse or even a phrase. Something to hang on to, tethered to eternity somehow: a priceless treasure.

As I weigh the Psalms just now, I realize how being immersed in them, or being embraced by them, could help so many of us in a culture of counterfeit spirituality. A thin, ideological kind of faith can wrap itself in a rah-rah, go-America, God's-on-our-side kind of religiosity. And then there's the self-indulgent spirituality that's all about me, with God pitching in to give me a boost with my pet projects. The Psalms will hack you out of a bogus, simplistic, mechanical, and ultimately disappointing relationship with God, and show you the path to the real thing, tougher, but substantial and life-giving.

Words to God Become the Word of God

What are the Psalms? Just a long collection of prayers that cry out, give thanks, plead, ponder, praise, and speak with God in surprising and profound ways. Most were sung, and from memory. Thankfully, they landed in the Bible, not because they are *about* God, but because they are directed *to* God. And when we read and speak them aloud now, they reveal to us what we'd never noticed or what we'd feared to notice about ourselves. I could deliver a lecture on what the Psalms were and are. But there's no substitute for reading them, slowly and quietly.

Theologians, poets, and preachers have characterized the Psalms as a great many amazing things, from a mirror of the soul to a school of prayer, from a little Bible to the manna of the church. I am fond of what Thomas Merton suggested: "The Church indeed likes what is old, not because it is old but rather because it is 'young.' In the Psalms, we drink divine praise at its pure and stainless source.... The Psalms are the songs of men who knew who God was.... For God has willed to make Himself known to us in the mystery of the Psalms."[1]

As an evil storm was descending over Europe in 1939, Dietrich Bonhoeffer called the Psalms the "prayerbook of the Bible." The Psalms can stand as the answer to what the disciples asked of Jesus: "Lord, teach us to pray" (Luke 11:1). But don't we just blurt out whatever we wish for God to do or hear? Bonhoeffer observes how easy it is to "confuse wishes, hopes, sighs, laments, rejoicings—all of which the heart can do by itself—with prayer." For him, prayer isn't just pouring out your heart. Rather, to pray is "to find the way to God and to speak with him, whether the heart is full or empty."[2]

Shrewdly, Bonhoeffer points out that children don't just start talking. They take up the language of their parents. And so we take up God's language—and that is how we pray. God's language of prayer is opened to us in the Psalms. Yes, they were at first words to God, those hopes, sighs, laments, and rejoicings. But under the superintending vigilance of God, these words *to* God become for us the Word *of* God.

It's eye-opening then to ponder how we make sense of the inspiration of the Bible. How is a psalm inspired? Literal factuality makes no sense for a psalm. The human element in our inspired Bible is nowhere more evident than in the Psalms. People who were hurting, scared, fretting, guilty, hopeful, giddy, and confused spoke out loud to God. Others, similarly wounded, anxious, and grateful treasured these words and prayed them too—and some were eventually written down. The Israelites kept collecting and reusing prayers, probably revising and improving them along the way, until part of what it meant to be an Israelite was that these were the prayers they all prayed. They learned to pray, to worship, to cope, to survive with these prayers. When they finally settled on what all should be in sacred Scripture, how could these prayers, made sacred by being prayed so long by so many, be left out?

I wish I knew more, or much at all, about the psalmists, the poets who first prayed these remarkable prayers. I suspect they would fit Niall

Williams's probing thought: "Poets do not escape into other worlds, they go deeper into this one. And because depths are terrifying, there is a price."[3] Can we overhear in these psalms their personal terrors, depth, and cost? I know I feel all of that in my life—and the Psalms get me in touch with all that, providing the words I need to express what otherwise might leave me speechless and floundering.

Dismantling and Remaking a World

In the Psalms, we discover a rich theology and a deadly serious tackling of issues we still face personally, socially, and politically. No one has articulated how they function better than Walter Brueggemann: "The Psalms not only propose and constitute a world; they intend also to unmake, deconstruct, and unmask other worlds which seduce and endanger Israel."[4] We'll see how that unfolds in the psalms we'll explore. All the psalms together invite us to look closely at the world as we know it. Like a wrecking ball, they knock down what is wobbly, so flimsy are the foundations. And then new footings are laid, and a fresh, trustworthy, hopeful structure rises from the ground. Deconstruction, then reconstruction. Disorientation, then reorientation.

In this little book, I'll ask you to trust me as we explore just 6 of the Bible's 150 psalms together. How did I select them? I'd hoped for a little set that together would be representative of the Psalter as a whole. But in my heart of hearts, I can confess that these six are my favorites—although there are four or seven or eleven others I adore just as much.

Thomas Merton had the intriguing notion that God likes it when you have a favorite psalm. Your favorite might change during a lifetime, and God uses that favorite during a particular season to speak deeply with you or for you to speak and listen deeply with God. Yet I'll always chuckle when I remember asking Sister Dianne Bergant, a brilliant Psalms scholar, "What is your favorite psalm?" With a hint of chiding in her voice, she replied, "All of them."

A Word on Translation

I hope our study of these six psalms will stir in you a love for all of them. I'll be working from the Revised Standard Version (RSV), admittedly from a previous generation. And why? Frankly, it's quite good, although I'll explore the Hebrew original with you and touch on what more recent translators have offered us. Most recent translations have aimed for a more colloquial, chatty, common kind of English. I'm not bugged by this. But it's noteworthy, to me at least, that the Hebrew we find in the Bible, especially in the Psalms, was not the colloquial, chatty, common Hebrew of the day. Scripture writers aimed higher, for a more elevated style, probably thinking their stories and songs were about God and for God, so reaching slightly upward on the quality-of-language scale made good sense.

One peculiarity of the RSV is that when God is addressed—and that happens a large percentage of the time in the Psalms—pronouns for God cling to the Thee and Thou familiar since the King James Version. A lawyer once complained to me that he couldn't understand the Bible, asking if a modern version instead of the King James his parents had given him might help. I laughed and said, "You lawyers specialize in devising complex wording in documents we have to hire a lawyer to understand. That King James made perfect, profound sense to my grandparents, who never spent a day in college!"

Feel more than free to consult, read, and pray any version of the Psalms you prefer! Just be sure you read and pray. And so, let us begin now with Psalms 8, 27, 51, 73, 90, and 116. The order is numerical, although I detect this order also makes sense thematically. But read them in any order you like. And when you're done, try your hand at some of the other 144!

1
Psalm 8

Awe:
When I
Look at the
Heavens

1

Psalm 8

Awe: When I Look at the Heavens

We do not often wonder about the location or time of day when Bible passages were originally composed. When we read Psalm 8, we probably do so indoors, in a well-lit room. Rather wonderfully, our psalmist was outside, at night, in the dark, gazing up into the night sky. "When I look at thy heavens, the work of thy fingers, the moon and the stars which thou hast established" (v. 3). Should you take a flashlight or your phone and ponder it in your backyard tonight?

There is a remarkable statue of St. Francis of Assisi high on a mountain just outside his hometown. Francis is lying flat on the ground, looking up, the way he often slept and prayed all night. His night sky, like Jesus's, was bright, glistening with too many stars to count, a dense array of pinpoints of light, the occasional flurry of meteors—unlike ours, ruined by the artificial, ambient light that blots out our vision. Francis usually opened his prayers by addressing God as "most high, glorious God." How often, as he slept outside on that high mountain, did he contemplate Psalm 8?

Awe

What the psalmist was filled with, what Francis thrilled to, and what might even happen with us is that elusive three-letter word: *awe*. A while back, a friend who knew me well urged me to read a book I'd have never found on my own: *Awe: The New Science of Everyday Wonder and How It Can Transform Your Life* by Dacher Keltner. What a gift. What a glorious surprise. What theological wisdom in a book not at all dedicated to God or religion!

What is awe, anyhow? It is whatever transcends your current understanding of the world, what moves you, rendering you not just speechless but also emotionally overwhelmed. It might be beauty or vastness, courage or kindness, a crescendo in a symphony that makes you want to rise from your seat, or a Special Olympics victory. Keltner interviewed people all over the world, asking about moments of awe, and he noted what was *not* mentioned: "Money didn't figure into awe....No one mentioned their laptop, Facebook, Apple Watch or smartphone. Nor did anyone mention consumer purchases, like their new Nikes, Tesla, Gucci bag or Montblanc pen. Awe occurs in a realm separate from the mundane world of materialism, money, acquisition and status signaling."[1]

I love that Keltner suggests "it is hard to imagine a single thing you can do that is better for your body and mind than finding awe

outdoors"[2]—which is precisely where Psalm 8 takes us by the hand
and leads us. The night sky. Enough to ponder for a lifetime. And we
have the added benefit of those fantastic telescopes, the Hubble and
the Webb, showing us what even Jesus and Francis could not begin to
glimpse or imagine. Yet their minds were blown in ways ours are not.
Can we recover a sense of awe? And why does it matter?

Spurgeon cleverly spoke of Psalm 8 as "the song of the astronomer."[3]
I knew one—a neighbor named Ralph who was a professor of
physics. He would call me at odd hours (10 p.m., midnight, once
at 3 a.m.), giddily urging me to walk over to his backyard, where
he had a telescope set up for me and my kids to join him in eyeing
some marvel: an alignment of the moons of Saturn, a distant comet,
the space station plugging along. One warm night, with a remarkable
tone of peace and joy, he told me, "Doing this makes me feel at home
in the universe."

In ancient times, people believed that the stars made music as
they traversed the night sky. A cynic might be right in arguing that
they do not. But is there music up there? Can the sky, however quietly,
praise God? Thomas Merton wrote, "A tree gives glory to God by
being a tree."[4] Don't the stars give glory to God by being stars?

It was on the starriest of nights when the shepherds heard the
angels sing. Did those shepherds contemplate Psalm 8 at night or even
on that first Christmas night? The stunningly beautiful backdrop to
the manger in Bethlehem was the night sky above, with its stars—and
the star! Did Psalm 8 drift into the minds of Mary and Joseph on that
holiest of nights, when Jesus cried out in the dark?

> *Thou whose glory above the heavens is chanted*
> *by the mouth of babes...*

> *what is man that thou art mindful of him,*
> *and the son of man that thou dost care for him?*
> *Yet thou... dost crown him with glory and honor.*
> *(Psalm 8:1-2, 4-5)*

A Cure for Despair and Anxiety

Awe is humanity's most precious ability. Cockroaches and squirrels apparently do not look up and hold creation in a dumbfounded awe. Is this capacity for awe part of our being created in God's image? I know that for me, when awe happens, usually catching me by surprise, I feel like... myself, my truest self that gets lost sometimes.

Awe, perhaps especially of the night sky, has curative powers. Jonathan Haidt wrote an alarming wake-up call of a book, *The Anxious Generation*, warning of the afflictions we're suffering from excessive smartphone and screen time. His remedy isn't just to shut them off but also to get outside and to do a lot of looking up. A wise friend once suggested to me that the antidote to despair is praise. Psalm 8, not accidentally, finds itself smack-dab in the middle of a thicket of ten complaint psalms crying out to God in sorrow, anxiety, pain, harassment, and adversity (Psalms 3–13). Was the editor of the book of Psalms subtly offering us a prescription for how to cope with and rise above preoccupations, suffering, and worry? Look up. Get outside. At night. Let your jaw drop in awe.

Awe takes time; it demands that we are still and curious. It's a matter of pondering, not just seeing, but dwelling on what you see, letting it seep deep into your soul, cherishing it in your mind, asking fresh questions, and listening with your heart. When the psalmist exclaimed, "When I look at thy heavens" (v. 3), the verb *'ereh* isn't just "look," as in glancing quickly. It's "look," "see," "consider," "gaze"—or "ponder." I'm reminded of the hymn "When I Survey the Wondrous Cross." You don't just glance at it or take a quick photo. You survey the thing. You measure. You contemplate how this came to be, what lies underneath, and what the consequences might be. You look and keep looking. You let your soul open up. You get a little lost in wonder, love, and praise.

You don't have to be a religious or spiritual person to be in awe or to be cured a little by the night sky. But consider the added, deeper, truer dimension of the psalmist's invitation to us to let it all be wrapped up in the arms of God. A while back, I visited Niagara Falls with a pastor-theologian friend. We noticed people around us snapping photos with their phones, bellowing out one-word exclamations like "wow," "geez," and "amazing." One guy kept muttering a four-letter word beginning with *f* that I won't repeat here. My friend told me what happened when our mutual friend, a rabbi, took his children to the Grand Canyon. Amid all the photo-taking and one-word yelping, the rabbi and his family bowed their heads and recited together a prayer they'd always known: "Blessed are you, King of the Universe, Creator of Wonders." Do you see the difference?

The Name of Our Lord

The psalmist has good words and provides us with good words for our awe. "O LORD, our Lord, how majestic is thy name in all the earth!" Notice, it's not just "O LORD." The psalmist lingers and grows more affectionate. "O LORD"—oh, and yes, "Our Lord." It's personal.

There's a relationship. It's not possessive either. And it's not singular. "My Lord"? Sure, but join hands with me; let's ponder and delight in this together. "Our Lord."

Who's included in that "our"? The rabbi and his family, my friend and I, but maybe also those who aren't around just now, those who've gone on to be with "our Lord" and enjoy eternal intimacy with "our Lord." Maybe even those who don't believe or who never look up. "Our Lord" is their Lord too. And never lording it over them or us or even the night sky. Our Lord is always good, generous, tender, never coercive, abounding in mercy. We're looking up into the depths of that mercy when we ponder that night sky.

You have to love the adjective "majestic" in verse 2, which just doesn't apply to even the most expensive trinkets we can buy. "Majestic" you reserve for the Swiss Alps or the Scottish Highlands or a newborn's stubby fingers or your grandmother's wrinkled smile. What's majestic here? "Thy name." Yes, the Israelites out of reverence added "the name of" to "the Lord" when we might simply say "the Lord." But let's reflect upon that name.

Or names. There are so many names for God in Scripture— as is fitting, God being God, God's being so large and mysterious and complex. I'm just James. But God is God, Lord, Most High, Wonderful Counselor, Everlasting Father, Prince of Peace, Immanuel, El Shaddai, Abba, the Word—on and on. The name in Psalm 8, so marvelous as to bear repeating in its very first verse, is YHWH (Hebrew having only consonants!), which we say out loud as Yahweh, a name so sacred to the Jews that when they came upon it in reading, they would substitute Adonai. Yahweh. God revealed this majestic name to Moses in Exodus 3. It means...well, what does it mean? Yahweh explained to Moses that "I am who I am," which is either no explanation at all or a singularly spectacular, mysterious, and ultimately truthful explanation!

The *y* is a clue that Yahweh is a verb. This Yahweh isn't a still life but something happening, in motion. The *a* is a clue that this verb is causative. Yahweh causes things—all things!—to happen. And the *y* is also a clue that this verb that is our Lord is future tense. Yahweh is the God who will be. Yahweh is our future.

Indeed, Yahweh's "glory" is "above the heavens," larger even than the furthest distance in the night sky. The psalmist and St. Francis would have known that was pretty darn far. Thanks to astronomy, we can be even more awed by the vastness of the Lord who's larger than that sky, since scientists tell us that the little pinpoint of light up there is a gigantic fireball, bigger than our sun, whose light has been hurrying toward us at—yes—the speed of light for thousands or millions of years. I can't wrap my mind around this, but I am in awe.

Why Bother with Us?

And the thought of it makes me feel small. Haven't you felt, as I often have, tiny, insufficient, insignificant, or not enough? The psalmist felt small, and wrote about it, sang about it, I think as a gift to us, inspired by God, words to God becoming the Word of God. "When I look at thy heavens, the work of thy fingers, the moon and the stars which thou hast established, what is man that thou art mindful of him, and the son of man that thou dost care for him?" (vv. 3-4). Modern translations have struggled with and tried to improve upon that word man, males being only half of us down here.

The NRSV and the CEB land on "human beings," which is accurate enough, as is Eugene Peterson's *The Message*: "Why do you bother with us?" What's lost when we update "man" to "human beings" is that the psalmist doesn't just feel small. He (or she!) also feels lonely.

There are so many reasons to feel small. There's simple math, of course. I am five feet, ten inches tall, and so I occupy 0.0005 percent of the space between the ground and the earth's ozone layer. If I calculate that to the sun or distant stars, we'd fill the rest of this book with zeroes after the decimal. I am indeed small. But I think about my utter insignificance. Around town I see thousands of cars in traffic, each with someone inside with a world of trouble and feelings. Do I matter amid the throngs? And that's just my city. As a pastor, I have an allegedly high-impact job. But does the little I do really nudge the world very far?

Am I enough? Not, do I have enough? But, am I enough? People with lots and lots feel they aren't enough. Do I matter—really? The psalmist was out in the dark, very small and alone. Down very low indeed. A friend of mine once went radio silent for about a month. I kept texting and calling. Finally, he responded with these cryptic words: "I fell in a hole and couldn't get out."

Quite a few psalms give voice to this mood of having fallen into a deep hole, especially Psalm 130: "Out of the depths I cry to thee, O Lord." Henri Nouwen, writing during his own darkest days, reminds us "There is a deep hole in your being, like an abyss. You will never succeed in filling that hole, because your needs are inexhaustible."[5] There's an emptiness, a loneliness that dogs us, even if you own a lot, even when you find yourself in a crowd, rubbing elbows at a party, or even at the dinner table with your spouse. Waking up at 3 a.m. and trying to quell the voices of worry or worthlessness is so exhausting. I wonder if that's why God gave us this psalm, set in the middle of the night.

How good of God to prompt the psalmist to ask the right question and to verbalize the question in just the right way: "What is man that thou art mindful of him, and the son of man that thou dost care for him?" (v. 4). Or for the lonely woman, "What is woman that you are mindful of her ... that you care for her?" Two lovely gifts are tucked inside this question. The first is that the psalmist even raises the question. It doesn't occur to cockroaches and squirrels to ask. We are made in God's image, which is why we ask and wonder. Even those who aren't very spiritual or religious wonder about belonging in the universe. We wonder if there's some "thou" out there.

Mindful? Care?

And then the answer is implied in the question in those two tender words, *mindful* and *care*. This psalmist isn't Job, who is talking with God—which is good—but can't stop hurling accusations that God doesn't care. Here we hear a puzzled, How could you, a God of such mind-boggling vastness, with a whole universe to tend to, and seemingly so very, very far away ("above the heavens"!), pay attention to, listen to, be mindful of, and even care for me? Peeling back the layers of darkness, peering closely upon those pinpoints of light, we begin to believe, to trust, even to know.

And it's not the strength of our faith or piety that gets us there. Nouwen understood, in his own deepest abyss, that God is faithful to God's promises. He adds this remarkable, hopeful notice: "Before you die, you will find the acceptance and the love you crave.... There is nothing to hold on to but this promise."[6] Before you die, you've got time. This reassurance, the way stars are trustworthy to show up and shine? We call that grace. And hope. "Even the darkness is not dark to thee," as another psalm (139:12) prays for and with us. "The light shines in the darkness, and the darkness has not overcome it" (John 1:5). Maybe this is why raising candles during "Silent Night" on Christmas Eve moves us so. There must be a God.

The psalmist offers no proof. Only faith, hope, and love. A dream in the night. It's aspirational. And so hopeful. We can embrace the dark. Daniel Snyder, a pastor and therapist, has observed how "we humans have devised a nearly infinite number of ways to keep the lights on in the dark, to put a comfortable face on mystery, to wrap the simple facts of beauty and suffering, love and loss, life and death in reassuring platitudes." But we need not dodge the darkness. Only by sitting in the darkness and learning to see in the dark can healing come. "The hours spent in prayer in the deepest part of the night tend to strip away defenses.... In those dark hours I found a bottomless stillness where it was impossible to deny my human fragility, my inevitable death, and my dependency on mysteries beyond my ability to comprehend. I also found the voice of my longing in the psalms."[7]

However small we may feel, especially in the dark, the psalm seems to declare the words of "Jesus Loves Me, This I Know": "Little ones to him belong." Niall Williams tells of a boy growing up a century ago in County Clare, Ireland. He loved the night. "When darkness fell, it fell absolutely, and when you went outside the wind sometimes drew apart the clouds and you stood in the revelation of so many stars you could not credit the wonder and felt smaller in body as your soul felt enormous."[8]

God Is Watching Us

We might flip the image. Rather than for the small one looking up, what's it like for God looking down? Okay, we know God's not "up there," but work with me. What is it like for God, looking back at us as we look up? As a boy, obsessed with astronauts and space, I doled out my hard-earned paper route earnings to buy that great photo Michael Collins took of the Apollo 11 lunar lander above the moon's surface with earth beyond. In her thoughtful novel *Orbital*, Samantha Harvey muses on the idea that he'd snapped a photo of every human being: "Only one is missing, he who made the image."[9] She meant Collins, but it made me chuckle, as I thought for a second she meant God!

But what about the people on the other side of the earth? Or those blanketed in night, or beneath clouds? God has Superman vision, looking right through clouds and darkness and the solid earth, spotting me, you, and the others who aren't even looking up, zooming in with loving oversight. God's eyes must be unfathomably complex yet simple, simultaneously seeing me, you, the stranger next door or around the world, peeking deep inside, cherishing, rooting for each one and all of us together.

Collins's photo is of our home, everybody's home, and all the joys, sufferings, dreams, history unfolding, like a tiny house we have to squeeze into together—so we've got to be gentle, generous, forgiving, and laugh easily, in awe of God, this place, and one another. Do you know Bette Midler's song "From a Distance"? From way out there, it's all beauty, harmony, and plenty. Her chorus reminds us that "God is watching us." Harvey's *Orbital* is about astronauts circling Earth, gnawed at by the dissonance between the beauty from up there and the troubles below. "You feel yourself pulled in two directions at once. Exhilaration, anxiety, rapture, depression, tenderness, anger, hope, despair" and "a desire to protect this huge yet tiny earth."[10] Doesn't God feel this dissonance, watching us? Doesn't God long to protect us down here and for us to share in caring for the place?

Small yet Integral

Back to the psalmist looking up. Acknowledging and confessing your smallness will shield you from that malady of pride. Looking up, asking, "Why do you bother with us?" will deflate any puffed up-ness—which is the great enemy of spirituality and relationships. To know I am small, vulnerable, and dependent is the opening to healing from God and among others.

Yes, I'm small, but it's a *we* who are small. *Our* Lord! Small but beloved—like so many small things: a child, a flower, a piece of cake, a kiss, an old photograph, a light on the Christmas tree, a candle, a memory, the pill you take to stay alive, that ring you wear, a smile, a hug, and your heart in your chest. My niece Katy, a rock climber who works in search and rescue at Yosemite, knows the outdoors intimately. She told me that "nature gets us in touch with the fact that we are small and yet integral. Every little piece matters." Mother Teresa, after showing up too late for her speech at a world hunger conference because she had stopped to feed one hungry person, explained, as she often did: "What we do is nothing but a drop in the ocean. But if we didn't do it, the ocean would be one drop less."[11]

Maybe, instead of looking for a big God, a powerful, authoritarian, dominating God, or for a God who enlarges us, large enough to grant our large wishes, strong enough to protect me and mine or to shove aside whatever threatens or confuses us, we think small. The psalm that starts so very big ("When I look at thy heavens") is the very psalm that then gets small and escorts us to a very small place, to meet and connect with a God who comes low enough and small enough to embrace us.

There's a single word in Psalm 8 that makes my soul soar. Are you as surprised as I am when you read just past "When I look at thy heavens" and find "the work of thy fingers"? God made the stars and moon and vast expanse of space—with God's *fingers*? Peter Craigie infers that the psalmist is dabbling in hyperbole to prod us toward a glimpse of God that is even larger than we'd imagined: "In contrast to God, the heavens are tiny, pushed and prodded into shape by the divine digits."[12] Indeed.

But on the other hand (literally!), picturing God with fingers invites us to ponder a God who is personal (so not just some blind Big Bang burst of energy) and even tender. Michelangelo frescoed God's fingers as strong but gentle, waving the heavens into being, reaching out for Adam with a gentle touch of an index finger. Showing mercy on the woman "caught in adultery," Jesus bent down and with his finger wrote in the dust, the earth from which God made us. Our fingers do our loveliest work, writing a love note, turning a soufflé in the pan, planting a flower, strumming a guitar, pointing out something amazing to a child, or wearing your grandmother's ring. When a baby is born, by cultural habit or some innate impulse, we count the little fingers. Ten! A miracle. When you were born, your mom or maybe your dad offered a gentle finger, which your tiny, stubby fingers grasped, the first and gentlest embrace of so many to come.

The Newborn's Fingers

Let's linger on this vision of a newborn's fingers and that gentle, loving embrace. Our psalmist, when exuding joy and admiration over "how majestic" is the name of "our Lord," adds that our Lord's "glory above the heavens is chanted by the mouth of babes and infants." Why not just "babes" or just "infants"? A poetic flourish? Did God prompt the psalmist to add the second to be sure every babe and every infant of whatever sort would be included? Do infants "chant" the glory of our Lord? What happier sound could there be than that first cry of a newborn, announcing to the world "I'm here"? What sweeter melody has ever been heard than the cooing and gurgling of a newborn? Don't they give more glory to God than the grandest massed choirs in fabulous churches?

Now we are getting to the very soul of the gospel. We're venturing into God's holy intentions that the psalmist didn't know about, or at least not yet (in his life on earth back then). The God whose glory is revealed in that vast array of stars and galaxies did God's very best work—or we should say, God showed us God's very best self—in the cry of an infant, *the* infant. God wanted us to know God's heart, and so God became what every one of us once was: an infant. God became small so that those of us who feel small under that expansive night sky might feel loved and then love that God who chose to become small. An infant asks of us what God asks of us: to be loved, to be treated tenderly, to share in the joy of simply being.

An infant is vulnerable, which was certainly the case back in Bible times! Barbara Brown Taylor preached a lovely sermon, imagining the moment the angels were told God's plan to step down into time to become a baby.[13] They objected. *Too dangerous down there! Insufficient security measures!* They thought God should save us in some safer way. But God, being the kind of God we now know, planned things so that the only way to redemption, the only plan that could truly save us from the inside out, the only way those who feel small would feel not small but very close to God was to become one of us, to be with us, with the ultimate goal that we would become like God. The psalmist, grasping after the big truth he could only dream of and yearn for, dared to suggest, "You have made man a little less than God." Not much less either!

When the Hebrew Bible was rendered into Greek, the translators squirmed over this and so morphed "little less than God" into "little less than the angels." They whiffed on the Hebrew, but we recall what happened a few decades after. God's glory above the heavens was indeed chanted, first in that initial cry of baby Jesus (which Madeleine L'Engle suggested sounded like the ringing of a bell!),[14] and then in the great choir of angels who came down from heaven to sing to those shepherds. After announcing the good news of the birth of the Savior, the angels sang, "Glory to God in the highest" (Luke 2:14)—as if they were riffing on this very psalm!

The Son of Man

Notice another detail in Psalm 8. "What is man that thou art mindful of him, and the son of man that thou dost care for him?" (v. 4). An ancient Israelite would have heard this as a clever, lovely poetic couplet, "son of man" back then just being another way to speak of a mortal person. But Christian ears perk up, don't they, when we hear "son of man"! The psalmist wasn't predicting Jesus, the Son of Man, coming centuries later and crying out in the dark, accompanied by a choir of angels. And yet, the profound insight of the psalmist, feeling small but not alone in the cosmos, hanging onto the hope and reality of God's intimate presence, had to be something of an unwitting hunch of what God ultimately was up to with us. A fair reason to cling to "What is man?" instead of "What are human beings?" or "What is humanity?" You lose not just the isolation that lonely one felt back in the day. You also lose the subtle tease God inspired into the psalm that the one down here who connects us with the heavens and God up there is none other than Jesus.

And let's roll a little further with "the son of man that thou dost care for him." Yes, God cared about Jesus, of course. And God's care for him was enacted by his mother. Mary cared for Jesus by sheltering him in her womb for months. Then, after hearing his first cry, she held him close, nursed him, cooed at him, and sang lullabies. I am always moved by that holy, tender circle of Mary's gentle embrace of her son, God's son. So much beauty.

You, like everybody else, once were in that same small circle of tender love. Someone encircled you with her love and adoration. You've never been closer to God than in that holy moment. You've never been more like God. We don't have to defy gravity and ascend to God. God has come down. The exponential expanse of God is measured by the smallness of Christ come down in the infant Jesus— just as your parents' very busy and spread-out world shrank when you were born.

There is so much more that could be said about God's gift to us in this eloquent psalm. The first to find the Christ child were outdoors at night: the shepherds and then the magi. Astrologers! A bogus sham of an art—and yet God will do whatever it takes to reach any and everybody. The heavens proclaimed even to those foreign diviners the glory come down.

Let's also notice that the climax of Jesus coming down to redeem us occurred when he entered Jerusalem to open what we now think of as Holy Week. Pressured by religious authorities nervous over the joyful acclaim of large crowds as he rode that donkey on Palm Sunday, Jesus responded by quoting our psalm, specifically verse 2: "Have you never read, 'Out of the mouth of babes and suckling thou hast brought perfect praise'?" (Matthew 21:16).

I wonder if Mary, Jesus's mother, was in that palm-waving crowd. Like all Jewish mothers, she had taught the Psalms to her children at an early age. Just a few days later, she would hear her beloved son recite two other psalms she had taught him, as he breathed his final breaths in agony from the cross: "My God,... why hast thou forsaken me?" (Psalm 22:1) and "Into thy hand I commit my spirit" (Psalm 31:5). Before all the troubles in Jerusalem, back at home in Nazareth, had Jesus and his mother ever taken an evening stroll, paused, looked up, and recited Psalm 8 together?

Or we could rewind to the top and reflect on the psalm's inscription: "For the choirmaster, according to The Gittith." Thank God for choirmasters who wave their arms to lift our choirs and congregations to praises that are just a little less than the angels. And the gittith was likely a musical instrument; we thank God for those as well. God's creativity is joined to the creativity God has instilled in us down here to design and craft beautiful and beauty-making things: a guitar, a pipe organ, an oboe, a drum—and then these are played with divinely gifted skill to assist us in proclaiming the glory of the God who is pleased and honored by such things.

For now, we end not just where the psalm begins but where it also ends. Verse 1 is repeated word for word in verse 9, as if the psalmist put bookends around his outburst of praise to try to frame it for us and to keep us focused on what is larger and better and most healing for ourselves: "O Lord, our Lord, how majestic is thy name in all the earth."

2
Psalm 27

Beauty:
One Thing
Have I Asked

2

Psalm 27

Beauty: One Thing Have I Asked

If you were to ask me to turn to one moment in Scripture that never fails to move me, one that reminds me to slow down and breathe, one that reframes my sense of me and the world and God and why we're here, I could well lean toward Psalm 27:4.

One thing have I asked of the LORD,
that will I seek after;
that I may dwell in the house of the LORD
all the days of my life,
to behold the beauty of the LORD,
and to inquire in his temple.

These words give voice to what I long to be about. They resonate in me as my life's mission statement, although distractions, busyness, and toxic messages yank me away too easily. Martha, "anxious and troubled about many things," missed out on sitting at the Lord's feet with Mary, who somehow intuited that "one thing is needful" (Luke 10:41-42). Mary beheld the beauty of the Lord.

I was a bit surprised a few years back to be invited to speak at a conference of Pentecostal clergy. I was way more surprised and plenty envious when, during the opening (and very long) song, my host drifted away from what everyone else was singing. With his arms and eyes raised toward—the ceiling? heaven?—he muttered, over and over and over, "Oh Jesus, you are so beautiful. Oh Jesus, you are so beautiful." I'd spoken with Jesus that morning myself, but I'd said, "Jesus, my back hurts."

How would we "behold the beauty of the LORD"? And where? In church? Most of us haven't heard a lot about "beauty" in church. Too much talk about doing good, judging others, or whether we like the pastor. What if we went to worship with the expectation "to behold the beauty of the LORD"? Would my prayers be less "Lord, please do this for me" and more "O Lord, you are so beautiful"? Would my day out in the world be more peaceful and even joyful if I were often on the lookout for "the beauty of the Lord"?

We Were Made for Beauty

So let's take a deep dive into this marvelous verse and the rest of the psalm that is its home. Sad in a way, but we need to ask, What is beauty? Buried as we are under an avalanche of pretty and cute and impressive and shiny and purchasable things, not to mention the ugly, the tawdry, and scary stuff, it's hard to dig out and discover genuine beauty. Beauty isn't necessarily photogenic; you won't find it on social media. You can't possess it. It has no productive function. You can only "behold" beauty—not "hold" but "behold." You look and you keep looking or listening or smelling or tasting. The beauty of a winding stream back in the woods. The beauty of a cloud. The beauty of a breeze. The beauty of a phase of the moon. The beauty of an old song. The beauty of your aunt's peach cobbler. The beauty of tears. The beauty of your grandmother's wrinkled face.

Beauty is in the eye of the beholder, but it's not simply taste or preference. The spiritual life could be defined as a long training in learning to notice beauty we've been missing. A child plucks a dandelion out of the front yard and presents it to her mom. A friend opens a cigar box and shows you a tattered photo of his dad in his Army uniform. The sun rises—again!—and you witness a miracle, a gift of God's grace. You feel your heart beating, you hear the voice of your sister, and you notice the cat napping. You study an old painting, you light a candle, and you relish silence.

How good of God to dazzle us with so much beauty. God could have made a functional world without it, and we wouldn't even know what we'd be missing. When creating everything, God, the artist, ever extravagant, kept splashing a little beauty here and there, apparently because God loves beauty and knew we'd delight in it as well.

We are made for beauty like fish for the water, or birds for the air, or children for the playground, or worms for dirt, or your grandchildren for your lap, or your heart for your chest, or…We could go on all day! And we could fill dozens of massive volumes of books like this expounding on all the beauty that abounds all over the place. The least we can do in life is to try to notice—and we are responsible to preserve beauty. God is honored when we notice and protect what God made.

We would also understand and praise God all the more, since God not only thought up and crafted beauty. God *is* beauty. Beauty is God? Well, beauty ushers us very close to the mind and heart of God. And can you feel the mercy in beauty? Wesley Vander Lugt calls beauty "oxygen for a soul-crushing existence."[1] There is so much ugliness out there, even in our own heads and hearts.

Notice all the stress and terror in the verses leading up to and following Psalm 27:4! Evildoers, adversaries, and foes assailing and slandering! A host encamping, war arising—and even parents failing their children! The psalmist, after professing, "The LORD is my light and my salvation," asks, "Whom shall I fear?" (v. 1). The list grows long, doesn't it? So much to fear. Watch the evening news. Go for a checkup. Drive in traffic. Wait for the phone to ring. Absorb the election results. Try to get back to sleep at 3 a.m. Send your child to college. Trying to rid your jittery mind of fear is like playing Whac-A-Mole.

The psalmist invites us to stop and to breathe in that oxygen of beauty. The novelist Dostoevsky famously declared that "the world will be saved by beauty."[2] The world seems hell-bent on destroying what beauty there is. But realizing the beauty, learning together to be tender with the beauty that is—beauty is our only hope.

And we get little glimpses that keep hope alive. Christmas Day during World War I: one side lobbed a rum cake across no-man's-land, the other side hurled a beer back across, and soon German and Allied soldiers met in the middle and sang "Silent Night" together. Among the ruins of Sarajevo, cellist Vedran Smailović played every day for a month, and survivors were bolstered with hope. There's some moral demand in beauty, isn't there? That beauty inspires us to act in beautiful ways and to restore the wonder that was nearly crushed. No matter how many adversaries and evil foes the psalmist was coping with, he clung to hope: "I believe that I shall see the goodness of the LORD in the land of the living!" (v. 13).

Beautiful Savior

So the "one thing" our psalmist seeks isn't just to behold beauty, as noble and healing as that clearly can be, but "to behold the beauty of the LORD" (v. 4). One of my earliest childhood memories was waiting with my mother in the hallway of a church for my sister to come out of choir practice. Through the door I heard angelic voices singing "Fairest Lord Jesus," even breaking into two-part harmony (so lovely in my memory that I wonder now how such young girls could muster such a marvel). And so "Fairest Lord Jesus" is forever my favorite hymn, and it will be sung at my funeral. "Beautiful Savior...thee will I cherish....Glory and honor, praise, adoration, now and forevermore be thine."[3] I hope to spend eternity lost in wonder, love, and praise, seeing Jesus—no longer "in a mirror dimly" but "face to face" (1 Corinthians 13:12).

We fixate too narrowly on Jesus as dying for us or dashing off a miracle or two or teaching brilliantly—but not so much on his beauty. Dostoevsky, believing only beauty could save the world, suggested there is just one truly beautiful face, that of Jesus. Not that he had what we'd rank as movie-star good looks. There was something compelling, something beautiful in his being. Why else would fishermen, who'd just met him a minute earlier, drop everything—their livelihoods, known world and families—to traipse off after him to who knows where?

Why did that centurion, after sizing up Jesus's pierced, abused body hanging on the cross, shamed and gruesomely executed, conclude that "truly this was the Son of God" (Matthew 27:54)?

I love the way Augustine pondered all we might envision about Jesus: "He is beautiful in heaven, beautiful on earth; beautiful in the womb, beautiful in his parents' arms, beautiful in his miracles, beautiful in inviting to life, beautiful in not worrying about death, beautiful in giving his life and beautiful in the tomb, beautiful in heaven. Listen to the song with understanding, and let not the weakness of the flesh distract your eyes from the splendor of his beauty."[4] Oh, Jesus, you are so beautiful. Haunting. Alluring. Unsettling. Hopeful.

Of course, Jesus himself was constantly drawn into the beauty that was God his Father, the one he called Abba. How much beautiful, tender care, and strength are captured in that intimate name, which Jesus used instead of the wordy pile of long words the pious in those days used, like Eternal, Omnipotent, Omniscient, Royal, Ineffable, all of them true enough, yet missing out on the lovely closeness God enjoyed with Jesus and yearns for with us.

God's loveliness can be discerned on every page of the Old Testament too. When Moses asked to see God's glory, God hid him in the cleft of the rock and told him, "I will make all my goodness pass before you" (Exodus 33:19). God's goodness is the display of the beauty of God's mind and heart—in nature, in every occurrence of love, goodness strewn all over the place and throughout every day, in trees, a child's laughter, the taste of a sandwich, waking from sleep, the sunshine, the sound of church bells, a stranger's kindness—endless goodness, all over the place and throughout every day. Our psalmist, embattled and weary, found the way to "behold the beauty of the

Lord," (v. 4) understanding that "I shall see the goodness of the Lord / in the land of the living" (v. 13).

The Beauty of Sorrow

We might amend that to say I will learn to catch glimpses of the beauty of the Lord in places that aren't pretty, in what many (but never God!) might call ugly, in moments and things that at first blush strike us as the antithesis of beauty. Niall Williams tells of a man whose wife has just died: "The old man's eyes were beautiful in grief. They were a blue that could not be matched, both pale and deep, and in their tenderness of after-tears held the testimony of true love and could not be long looked at lest they break your heart."[5]

The inspiring documentary *Waste Land* takes us to the world's largest garbage dump, where the poor poke through the trash and create stunning art from the refuse, those treated like trash serving as models for beautiful portraits, their gathered trash transformed. The turning point in Francis of Assisi's life was in overcoming his natural revulsion when he encountered a leper; instead of bolting, he embraced and kissed the man. A beautiful leper.

The French painter Rouault is a favorite of mine among many who depict poverty and grief with a virtuosity that doesn't demonize but rather dignifies what we might pity; Sandra Bowden calls him a "visual prophet,"[6] portraying the disregarded and discarded, and Christ as one of them. Samuel Barber's *Adagio for Strings* has such a beautiful, poignant sorrow that it provided the perfect soundtrack for *Platoon*, a film about unspeakable violence and suffering in the killing fields of Vietnam. The National Memorial for Peace and Justice in Alabama, with its 805 hanging steel monoliths commemorating thousands of lynchings, has an eerie, haunting yet undeniable beauty. In Marilynne Robinson's *Gilead*, John Ames asserts that "there is a dignity in sorrow simply because it is God's good pleasure that there should be."[7]

And it's the paradoxical beauty of the Savior that reveals God's deft ways with ugliness: "His appearance was so marred.... He had no form or comeliness that we should look at him, and no beauty that we should desire him. He was despised and rejected by men; a man of sorrows ... and as one from whom men hide their faces he was despised" (Isaiah 52:14; 53:2-3). The one beautiful face that will save the world.

How Beautiful Is the Body of Christ

Jesus was the ultimate goodness of the Lord in the land of the living, Immanuel, God with us. When Jesus left, he didn't really leave. He left not a void but his own body, the Body of Christ. The opening verse of Acts looks back to the Gospel of Luke, which speaks of "all that Jesus began to do and teach." As his Body, we continue what Jesus began. That old poem often attributed to Theresa of Avila gets it right: "Christ has no body now on earth but yours, no hands but yours, no feet but yours."

Want to see a miracle? Want a vision of what God's mercy and power is like? Look no further than God's decision to use the church to be not a club or an institution but Christ's literal body walking around and doing good. Like all bodies, we can be awkward. We stumble. We have our troubles, blemishes, and weaknesses. But still, we are Christ's body.

Psalm 27 illustrates how the individual discovers true individuality by being part of the community, especially in prayer. Ellen Charry, showing us how to read closely, notices the way the psalmist addresses the congregation, then speaks directly to God, then back and forth a few more times. "One can almost see his human audience watching expectantly as he turns his body now toward them, now away from them, toward God, and back to them again. The rapid movements effectively impress upon the auditors how nearby God is and how easily beseeched."[8]

When the Body of Christ shares in prayer, when we embrace God's broken world, when we love out of our own brokenness, when we look more like a lamp set on a lampstand than a mimic of the world—when we live into Luther's vision of the beggar telling other beggars where to find some food, then we can truly sing that Twila Paris chorus, "How beautiful is the Body of Christ."[9] How beautiful were the Israelites who first heard and then continued to chant this psalm, along with monks and choirs and plain folk in churches throughout the ages.

In My Mother's House

Churches. Buildings. Frederick Buechner wisely suggested that "maybe the best thing that could happen to the church would be for some great tidal wave of history to wash it all away—the church buildings tumbling, the church money all lost, the church bulletins blowing through the air like dead leaves, and the differences between preachers and congregations all lost too. Then all we would have left would be each other and Christ, which was all there was in the first place."[10] Indeed. The beauty of the Lord in the people.

But thank God for the buildings. A place to come in out of the rain and attend to the things of God together. A quiet place to pray. Storage for our curriculum, hymnals, and paraphernalia. A wedding venue where you don't worry about the weather. A structure to cast its long shadow over the cemetery. A place of literal sanctuary, a place to flee for safety, under whose floorboards some Jews were rescued from the Nazis. A mute witness to a cynical world.

I love the moment in Lorraine Hansberry's *A Raisin in the Sun* when a daughter goes off to college and gets smart enough to come home over break and report to her family her very valid intellectual doubts about God. Her mother rises from her chair, crosses the room, slaps her daughter across the cheek, and says, "Now—you say after me, in my mother's house, there is still a God."[11] Church spires are no longer the tallest structures in our cities, but even in the shadows of skyscrapers, they do bear witness that there still is a God.

Our psalmist clearly is in the temple in Jerusalem. He asks for "one thing," but it's really two or three—maybe the way God is one but three, or what I want for Christmas is a camera that also needs a tripod and flash. His one wish is "that I may dwell in the house of the Lord all the days of my life." But then parts B and C of that wish, the way that the wish is spelled out and fulfilled is "to behold the beauty of the Lord, and to inquire in his temple" (v. 4). All that is a single thing: to be in the temple, to inquire (about which we'll say more later), and to behold the Lord's beauty.

The visible manifestation of the Lord's beauty, for the ancient Israelites, was the temple, an unsurpassable marvel, one that should have been the eighth wonder of the world. I try to fathom how breathtaking it was for pilgrims catching their first glimpse of that temple from the crest of Mount Scopus. They had traveled in caravans for many miles along dusty, rocky roads from plain gray towns where the only buildings were shabby, just a few rocks, some dirt, and thatch. Then this! The gleaming pavement, the elaborate architecture, soaring pillars and walls of ivory, and massive wooden columns of Lebanon cedar with coatings of bronze and gold that caught the sun's rays—enough to dazzle and nearly blind you. The glory of the Lord. The beauty of the Lord.

Worship in that temple was designed to induce awe and praise for the Lord whose house it was. The architects of Solomon's and later Herod's temples knew how to exploit light to heighten the beauty of the place, inside and out. Oriented toward the Mount of Olives in the east, high windows and the massive open doors would have let in the rising sun and its orange, luminous glow and emerging brilliance, especially as it glinted off the bronzed walls and colorful tapestries. The glory, the beauty of the Lord.

Light from Light

Of course, the Israelites associated God's glory with brightness, with an intense blaze of light, like that of the sun, before which you shield your eyes. Israel's neighbors thought of the lights in the sky as deities. Egyptians worshipped Aten, the sun god; Assyrians worshipped Sin, the moon god. Israel's God is far larger and mightier, sun, moon, and stars being yet a few more items God crafted in creation and which God guides across the skies for his pleasure and purposes. "The LORD is my light" (Psalm 27:1) bears witness to God's glory, exhibited dazzlingly in the sun's shining, which brings warmth, our ability to see, the marking of time, and photosynthesis so green things can grow.

Scripture never tires of riffing on light as a meaningful image for God. "The light shines in the darkness, and the darkness has not overcome it" (John 1:5). "I am the light of the world" (John 8:12). "Darkness is as light with thee" (Psalm 139:12). God's first word in creation was *light*, and at the consummation of all things, God's brightness will illumine everything, so we will need neither sun nor moon (Revelation 21:23-25). No wonder the Nicene Creed exalts Christ as "Light from Light."

Quite a few psalms praise God by praising the marvel of God's home on earth. "How lovely is thy dwelling place.... My soul longs, yea, faints for the courts of the LORD.... Even the sparrow finds a home ... at thy altars, O LORD" (Psalm 84:1-3). The psalmist wishes he could live there permanently. Yes, the architectural wonders staggered the senses. But it was the awareness of the Lord's palpable presence in such a place that elicited that longing. "For me it is good to be near God" (Psalm 73:28). Of course, the premise of Israelite religion was that you made pilgrimage to such a place so you'd carry it home in your heart and relish the recollection every day until you could return, thus living always with a keen sense of God's nearness.

Verse 6 speaks of prayer and sacrifice offered under God's "tent." The temple was the solid stone successor to the tent, the tabernacle Israelites worshipped in out in the wilderness. When we think of the beauty of God's special place, mobile like the tabernacle or fixed like the temple, we recall how ex-slaves who'd fled Egypt with nothing but the clothes on their backs managed to construct a beautiful, ornate tent for worship out in the wilderness. The night before they hurried out of Egypt, Moses told them to ask the wealthy Egyptians for gold and jewelry (Exodus 11:2), which they actually gave them, terrified as they were by the harrowing series of plagues.

What was the gold and jewelry for? Not for fashioning that golden calf (Exodus 32)! And not for their own pleasure. The gold and jewelry were intended for the Tabernacle. If we ponder the beauty of the Lord and the Lord's house, might it be that whatever precious items we've accrued could glorify God best not worn around our necks or dangling from our ears but by beautifying God's place and furthering the work of God in the world?

The Cathedral Was for God

Back to the buildings. How lovely were those small homes in Antioch, Philippi, and Ephesus where a handful of the very first Christian converts met for meals and prayers? As Christianity grew, Christians began to occupy massive basilicas in the cities, buildings originally dedicated to those pagan deities on Mt. Olympus who proved not to be deities at all. I love the repurposing of worldly buildings into houses of the Lord. I once worked on a renovation project in Lithuania for which we transformed a former Soviet recruiting station, which before that had been a staging area for the transport of Jews to concentration camps, into a church.

Medieval cathedrals leave me slack-jawed. How on earth did people eight hundred years ago build the most gargantuan, glorious buildings the world has ever seen? So much beauty, mimicking in their height and decoration the glory of God. Ken Follett's *The Pillars of the Earth* tells of a mason named Tom who realized while working on a cathedral "that the walls had to be not just good, but *perfect*. This was because the cathedral was for God, and also because the building was so *big* that . . . the merest variation from the absolutely true and level could weaken the structure fatally."[12] And I love that some of the most brilliant paintings and sculptures are so high up, or behind pillars, or even in the attics that mere humans visiting the cathedral could never see them—as was intended, for those works of art were exclusively for God. The Lord too loves "to behold the beauty of the Lord."

The acoustics in those cavernous spaces move me. I suspect worshippers in medieval times didn't fully understand much of what was going on due to distance and the reverb time—but also because services were conducted in Latin, which common folk did not understand. Their presence there, just like the hidden art, was for God. A church member of mine was very hard of hearing and then, over time, grew entirely deaf. Yet she kept coming for worship. When I wrote her a note to ask her why, since she couldn't hear my sermon or the choir or converse with friends, she wrote back to say she didn't come for me or music or the other people, but for God. And then she added that, in the silence, she found it easier to fix her mind on the Lord. "One thing I have asked of the Lord / . . . to behold the beauty of the Lord, / and to inquire in his temple" (Psalm 27:4).

As I drive through cities or around the countryside or travel abroad, I always take note of the churches and try to pause and offer a prayer of thanksgiving. Every one of them, a neo-Gothic stone throwback, a brick colonial with a steeple, a wooden A-frame on a rural road, a storefront, and even those modern hipster worship centers: how lovely is your dwelling place! I am beholding the beauty of the Lord in and through each one, a place built by the faithful for themselves but more for God.

Glory on Each Face

The beauty of the Lord is perhaps most fully on display not just in the lovely buildings and not only in the fellowship and mission of the people, but in each person, in myself and in you. In the sanctuary we sing, "Surely the presence of the Lord is in this place .... I see glory on each face." We are, each one of us, made in the image of God. Can you behold the beauty of the Lord in the Lord's people?

And not just in the beaming, manifestly spiritual face. Every face. The confused, the forlorn, the fun-loving, the wrinkled, and the newborn. Every face—and every body. Paul asks us, "Do you not know that your body is a temple of the Holy Spirit?" (1 Corinthians 6:19). Tall, short, skinny, heavy, growing, sagging, ravaged, photogenic, and bowed down: if we have the eyes to see, if we long to behold the beauty of the Lord, we develop spiritual eyes that can see the image of the Lord duplicated and multiplied in every person.

Starting with the one in the mirror. Hans Urs von Balthasar, in his lovely little book on prayer, opened by naming that we all have a sanctuary built within. It may be dusty and covered over with weeds, but we don't have to build it from scratch. Quite a few medieval theologians delighted in the thought that God's inhabiting the believer is nothing other than God's beautiful dwelling place on earth. Nothing puffed up about that. Wesley Vander Lugt notes how

"Beauty dislodges us from the center of the story"[13]—which is a relief, isn't it! The beauty of the Psalms recenters our identity, focus, and energy upon the Lord.

One Thing

Let's meander through a few other items in Psalm 27. The "one thing" the psalmist asks for in verse 4 is a complex "one." To "dwell in the house of the Lord" always, "to behold the beauty of the Lord," and "to inquire in his temple." That's the RSV reminding us that we enter worship not to consume or judge but to ask. Who has duped us into thinking faith is all about certainty when it's truer and healthier to think of our life with God as curiosity, a humility, asking for what we don't yet know?

The Hebrew verb rendered "inquire" is *baqēr*, the precise meaning of which no one is sure about. The NIV tries "to seek him." The CEB makes a big shift, so it's not God but the holy place: "constantly adoring his temple," echoed by the great Robert Alter, "to gaze on his palace."[14] I love it when we just aren't sure what the Hebrew means. God enjoys it when we scratch our heads and wonder. There's always a mystery in the text, especially when we're speaking of God! And don't we do this even in everyday English, especially in relationships that matter? What did she mean when she said...? I heard what he said, but I wonder if he was trying to tell me...

Eugene Peterson, in his paraphrase *The Message*, offers us "I'll study at his feet." Was he thinking about Mary in Luke 10:38-42, where "one thing" looms large? Martha in the kitchen doing what women were to do, Mary not only failing to help her beleaguered sister but defying custom by sitting at the rabbi's feet—a privilege reserved only for men! Surely, she expected Jesus to shoo Mary away and into the kitchen. But gently he invites Martha into a fresh space of mercy and possibility: "You are anxious and troubled about many things; one thing is needful. Mary has chosen the good portion" (Luke 10:41-42). Mary was beholding the beauty of the Lord; she was inquiring in the temple that he was.

The speaker in Psalm 27 was distracted by many troubles. Could it be that really just one thing is needful for him, for Martha, for us? Every wise therapist or spiritual guide is right to diagnose the trouble we suffer: a divided self. Healthy thoughts, negative thoughts, worldly thoughts, cravings, dreams, parental voices, and society's messages: we get frayed, and it's hard to focus, hard to be our true selves—if we can even discern that true self any longer. The primary goal of the spiritual life, God's dream in giving us the Psalms, is that over time, we will develop a kind of inner simplicity, a sort of spiritual gyroscope that keeps us pointed toward our true north. "One thing is needful" (Luke 10:42). "One thing have I asked" (Psalm 27:4). I've known people (and occasionally, by God's grace, I am momentarily one of them) who manage a peaceful and even joyful orientation even in the thick of racket or crises or hurry or weariness.

The question is whether we can trust Scripture and the saints when they suggest to us that the secret to life isn't "more," accumulating experiences and things. In the spiritual life—heck, just in life—less is more. The only way to slow things down is to slow down. You are enough. You have enough. You are here (as in on earth, in your life) for one thing, not many.

How many songs, poems, novels, miniseries, and movies dramatize the frustrations of not quite finding that one thing but then also the joys of finally finding the one thing? Dorothy comes home to Kansas. Ain't no sunshine when she's gone. Andy escapes Shawshank. The rich young ruler turned away sadly. Annie and Sam meet atop the Empire State Building. Even these come up a little short of beholding the beauty of the Lord, soaring now where Christ has led on Easter morning or being surprised by joy, the joy of mercy and hope. The pearl of great price for which you sell everything. Simply dropping your nets and following Jesus.

Grab hold of that one thing, and never let it go—or realize that one thing has a firm grasp on you. Then you have good cause to fulfill Psalm 27's final verse trifecta: "Wait for the LORD"—and you can, knowing God will in God's good time redeem you and all of creation. "Be strong"—and you are, for the beauty of the Lord is the Holy Spirit strong in you. "Take courage"—for

> *The LORD is my light and my salvation;*
> *whom shall I fear?*
> *The LORD is the stronghold of my life;*
> *of whom shall I be afraid?*
> *(Psalm 27:1)*

3
Psalm 51

Mercy: Create in Me a Clean Heart

3

Psalm 51

Mercy: Create in Me a Clean Heart

"Lord, teach us to pray" (Luke 11:1). Such was the request the disciples made of Jesus. They'd witnessed something special in his intimate connection to God and wanted in on it. Is prayer something we just do, as naturally as a child asking for a piece of cake or crying over a scraped knee? Or is it a skill, a hard-fought relationship that doesn't just happen but requires some learning and growth?

Dietrich Bonhoeffer, having assembled a little band of German Christians at odds with the Nazis and under intense harassment, prayed the Psalms with them and delivered lovely lectures on the Psalms in *The Prayerbook of the Bible*. His most arresting thoughts? Prayer isn't just wishing or even pouring out your heart before God. "Not what we want to pray is important, but what God wants us to pray." God might want us to pray what is *not* in our hearts, or what is contrary to our hearts. You learn a language by studying, listening, and then trying for yourself. So the Psalms provide for us God's language, which we absorb and then pray ourselves. "The richness of the Word of God ought to determine our prayer, not the poverty of our heart."[1]

If this is so (and we hope so, or else our prayer is nothing but "Gimme!"), then Psalm 51, beloved as it is for some of its familiar lines, will require of us some unlearning of what our hearts have absorbed from the culture, and some relearning of old habits of spirituality like the confession of sin, sacrifice, and forgiveness. We modern people have heard of such things, but we get confused and a bit laid back or even presumptuous about them.

Whatever Became of Sin?

"Cleanse me from my sin!" (Psalm 51:2). When I was a little kid, if you'd asked me, "What's the purpose of church?" I'd have guessed that it was the place where you admitted your sins since you were last there and asked God for (and received) forgiveness—hopefully with the determination to do better next week and not need so much forgiveness. Admittedly, I'd heard too much fiery Southern Baptist preaching that stirred up considerable terror in me. I felt much guilt; my parents motivated with guilt! But I didn't know much about God or sin.

What exactly is sin? Intentionally breaking God's rules? Perhaps we could ask not, What is sin? but, What *was* sin? In 1973, psychiatrist Karl Menninger published *Whatever Became of Sin?*—laying out his shrewd prediction that as we learn more and more about illness, psychology, heredity, dysfunction, biology, environment, and trauma, sin would gradually cease to be a plausible explanation of why we do and think what we do. Increasingly, talk of "sin" feels like dusting off some fossil from our religious past.

Donald Trump was asked, while running for president in 2016, if he ever asked God for forgiveness. Democratic-leaning Christians howled in sneering protest when he said, "No, I work hard, I'm an honorable person, I don't make mistakes, so I don't ask for forgiveness"—a far cry from Jimmy Carter's humble confession in 1976 that he had harbored lust in his heart. But Trump was, as usual, simply holding up a mirror so Americans could see themselves. Even churchgoers tend to think, *I'm a pretty good person; I do my best.* We don't come to worship to clear the air and make amends with God. We come to ask for God's help with our projects or to feel better or for an hour of spiritual entertainment.

Perhaps we should be grateful that sin has been forced to sit out in the hallway for a season. Menninger was right: back in the day, not knowing any better, we thought of schizophrenia, bipolar disorder, dementia, or postpartum depression as the product of sin or demon possession. How much harm was done? Kids from dysfunctional, abusive homes were castigated as sinful for their delinquent behavior. Weren't they crying out for help? How manipulative were the churches and their priests by threatening the torments of hell to motivate people to donate or do the church's self-indulgent bidding? Chris E. W. Green puts it well: "Nothing is more sinful than what we've said about sin, and what we've done in the name of our hatred for sin."[2]

Also, let's just acknowledge how our consumer society has muddled our thinking about God, sin, and goodness. For centuries, the church warned us about the Seven Deadly Sins: pride, greed, sloth, gluttony, lust, envy, and wrath. Nowadays, these describe the good life in America—and we might even pray for God to help us to achieve a life of comfort, plenty, pleasure, and the thrashing of the people who don't share our political ideology. If you found yourself lounging in a resort with a sumptuous spread and fine wine before you, stealing a kiss with your handsome lover, having outstripped your competitors in business, you might post a selfie, adding #blessed— and a pair of praying hands.

In the Bible's school of prayer, Psalm 51 is one of the Seven Penitential Psalms (seven? to counter the Seven Deadly Sins?): Psalms 6, 32, 38, 51, 102, 130, and 143. For over fifteen hundred years, Christians have looked to these seven to give voice to their sorrow for sin and their earnest pleas for forgiveness. I love it that Augustine, late in his life, bedridden, his eyesight failing, the Vandals laying siege to the city, had these seven psalms written on large canvasses in a very large font and had them hung around his bed so he could pray what God wanted him to pray during his final hours.

The Quality of Mercy

The title affixed to the top of Psalm 51 makes my head spin, as it reminds us of just how ugly Bible people can be. I promise we'll delve into David's appalling behavior shortly. For now, let's weigh the opening words of the psalm itself, which isn't about David but all of us: "Have mercy on me." That's our deepest gut need and our endless quest—and not just when we seek forgiveness for sin!

We need mercy always—always have, always will. The breath you just took is entirely by God's mercy. Before you were—at all!—you were mysteriously and miraculously dependent on God's mercy. You were just coming to be. And in your first home. The Hebrew word translated "mercy" is *rachamim*—from *rechem*, meaning "womb." You didn't earn your place there, nor did you take care of yourself there. Even after your mother bore you—at considerable cost to her own body, not yours—she sought nothing but good for you; she loved you fiercely. God's mercy is like a mother's tender care; her mercy *is* God's tender care.

Deep inside, don't you crave mercy?—to be loved despite your craziness, to be handled tenderly? Mercy never passes judgment. Mercy is never shocked by sin or suffering or anything at all in the reality of life. Mercy can't be earned and laughs at the very notion of earning. A vulnerable child hasn't earned his place in the family. Children are treated with gentle mercy and unconditional tenderness because . . . well, mercy needs no reasons.

Sure, later on you have to cry out for mercy. A kid was about to pound the daylights out of me on the playground—and I was required to say, out loud, "Mercy." A terrible, horrible mistake has been made, smashing a well-arranged life, and your regret is so intense that no strategy can extricate you from the mess. The only cry left to make is "Mercy." You gaze at the crucifix, and you keep looking, letting it nestle down into the marrow of your self, and finally you get it. Your only plea is "Mercy." And there's so much mercy in being able to seek that mercy.

Another Hebrew word translated "mercy" is *hesed*, which is steadfast, unshakably committed love. God sees our waywardness, but instead of being angry, God grieves, pursues, and does not rest until healing is achieved. God's mercy is nowhere more brilliantly displayed than when Joseph forgives his vicious brothers and even finds God's hidden hand bringing good out of evil (Genesis 45). Mercy works mightily, sometimes unnoticed, in the shadows, for good, even using human missteps and meanness for God's good ends. No wonder that great hymn sings of mercy as plural: "Morning by morning, new mercies I see."[3]

Merciful Commandments?

Mercy isn't only needed when God's commandments are broken. The commandments themselves are mercy. Don't covet? You don't have to, as God and God's blessings are enough already. Keep the Sabbath? You can rest, for the world doesn't depend on your feverish labors, but on God's mercy. How good of God to show us in mercy the way to a whole, joyful life! Jesus pressed the commandments further, not with a "Gotcha!" but with higher mercy. Don't kill? Don't let anger riddle your soul. Don't commit adultery? Don't be ensnared by lust. Jesus, so full of mercy, wishes to set us free from all that is toxic in our heads and hearts. He was fleshing out Psalm 51:6: "Behold, thou desirest truth in the inward being; / therefore teach me wisdom in my secret heart."

Mercy frees us to identify, understand, and feel genuine remorse for sin, and even to enjoy a merciful understanding of sin. Sin isn't merely breaking God's rules. It's more like James Allison's insight that all of us, "basically good, find ourselves inextricably caught up in an addiction to being less than ourselves."[4] Or, it's not so much that I mess up, and if I ask, God forgives. Rather, I *am* a mess.

These thoughts have helped me: Karl Barth suggested that sin is taking yourself too seriously. And so we can step back and chuckle at ourselves, shaking off a bit of sin. Christian Wiman told about taking his dog Mack for a checkup, and the doctor found the dog had been carrying a bullet inside his torso since before he came to live with Wiman. How disturbing, the reality that somebody was cruel enough to shoot this dog and leave him to crawl off and die. But somehow Mack had survived, yet in all his years in the Wiman household never complaining—"as if he'd learned that it does not pay…to let a human know what you feel."[5] Could sin be when you hide your brokenness and pain? Isn't sin more brokenness and pain than offense?

Can we widen our field of vision and grasp that sin and brokenness aren't merely solo problems. We dwell in a culture that is not of God, which grieves God's heart. We're enmeshed in it; we share society's troubles. I am a mess, and I am *in* a mess. Remember that the people of Israel gathered as a congregation and prayed Psalm 51. We can overhear Israel asking for mercy and forgiveness. We understand that today's church and world need mercy and forgiveness.

Psalm 51 speaks of bones that are broken. What is sin's impact on the physical body? Studies show that your body is forever impacted by big stressors in your childhood: being abandoned, parents divorcing, witnessing a murder, going hungry, or experiencing a home eviction. God grieves sin because God knows that when we live out of sync with the ways God has mercifully shown us, our bodies sustain damage. Can you count the ways? God's not mad. God steps into the breach, full of mercy, and invites us to healing and freedom by the power of God's Spirit.

David Had Gone in to Bathsheba

We might glide past the titles to most of the Psalms. But this one? It was "when Nathan the prophet came to him [David] after he had gone in to Bathsheba." No subtlety in that little word *in*. Check out the story in 2 Samuel 11–12. It will make you blush, and it serves as a diagnosis of what goes awry in all of us and in the people around us. Psalm 51 isn't merely how David tried to recover. The psalm is God's merciful path for you and me to recover from the messes we've made and the messes that we are.

It was spring, "when kings go forth to battle" (2 Samuel 11:1)— so why was David chilling in his palace while his army is out in the field? The second verse of this chapter begins with that enigmatic, suggestive "It happened . . ." Those two words are a clue that we're into something big. It didn't just "happen"! David saw a woman bathing. Nothing tawdry on her part. Today we can visit the archaeological site where David's palace once soared over a neighborhood of small homes—and today, just as back then, we notice people doing what they're doing on their flat rooftops. David inquired and then "took her" (2 Samuel 11:4). Don't miss the power differential, the seizure against her will. I call Bathsheba the patron saint of the #MeToo movement. David just took whatever he wanted. *He* needed mercy? How about Bathsheba?

Hard not to contrast this with Jesus, who similarly saw a woman alone, middle of the day, at Jacob's well (John 4). He could have "taken" her. But instead, he listened to her, cared for her, and empowered her. Was David's sin the physical act of seizing and forced intimacy? Yes. But wasn't his larger sin his failure to see her as a person, the way

Jesus saw the Samaritan woman, and listen to and respect her? Wasn't David inflicting his disordered self on her?

Deny, Deny, Deny

When his sophomoric dalliance resulted in pregnancy, David launched into cover-up mode. "Thou shalt not get caught. How do I cover my tracks?" Mind you, he needn't have bothered. Spurgeon is right: "No other king of his time would have felt any compunction for having acted as he did; hence there were not around him those restraints of custom."[6] As a king he could do as he wished. But he was still an Israelite, aware that at least among God's people, seizing somebody else's wife and siring a child would be shameful.

And so, he coaxed her husband home from battle. But Uriah was a far better man, refusing to go in to her; soldiers on short-term active duty were prohibited from sleeping with their wives—not by David but by God! Then we witness the height of arrogant, cynical cruelty: David jotted down a note to Joab, ordering him to put Uriah in the most vulnerable point in the battle so he'd be sure to be killed, and handed the note for Uriah himself to carry, probably chuckling to himself that Uriah was too much of a dope to peek inside. Lord, have mercy on Uriah.

Thinking he'd washed his hands of the matter, David was oblivious to the sorry truth that he had "done that which is evil in [God's] sight" (Psalm 51:4). God saw, even if the rest of the nation fell for the lie. And God is not mocked. There is, at the core of God's mercy, an accountability—this time in the form of Nathan. He didn't rumble in and accuse David. Rather, he told a story, supposedly about somebody else: a rich man seized the precious lamb of a poor man. With righteous indignation, David's temper flared over the mere possibility! Was David blind to the story being about him? Or was he in self-justifying mode already, clinging to the fantasy that surely Nathan could not know? But he knew: "You are the man" (2 Samuel 12:7). David's cockiness crumbled. The mighty king could only wallow in guilt.

Can we hear his greatest fear in our psalm? "Cast me not away from thy presence" (Psalm 51:11). Did he dare hope that God would not abandon him? God didn't abandon Adam and Eve even after casting them from Eden. God didn't abandon Cain east of Eden but marked his forehead as a sign of guilt but also divine protection. Hagar was cast into the wilderness by Abraham and Sarah, but God heard her cry out in dereliction and answered. God heard Jesus ask why he'd been abandoned on the cross. But after three days, God could not leave the beloved Son in the tomb any longer and raised Jesus up. "Cast me not away" is the prayer already answered before we pray it.

David Gets off the Hook?

The title of the psalm would have us think of David, full of remorse and realizing his sin, as the one praying and being forgiven. Okay. Sort of. But doesn't it kind of let David off the hook?—as if you can sin, and terribly, but if you are eloquently contrite and profoundly emotional in your remorse, all will be well? Prayers for mercy aren't about merely wiping the slate clean and getting out of hock with God. Mercy, the powerful, spiritually effective mercy of God, actually heals. It's like medicine for a sick soul.

David was a mess—as are we all. He had broken half the Ten Commandments (coveting, adultery, killing, false witness, and stealing), and maybe six if you count "No other gods," as David's god was clearly his bloated ego. Think of David and those Seven Deadly Sins! He's succumbed to six: lust, pride, sloth, greed, wrath, and envy...and maybe even gluttony. Is he just forgiven or also healed? What about the carnage, those forever devastated by his sin? Is there hidden divine healing and hope for them in this psalm?

I would propose that we walk through the whole psalm together, with David in the back of our minds, but also all of us in all times and places, not to mention our culture and the whole world. I love Spurgeon's remark: "This is the most deeply affecting of all the Psalms, and I am sure the one most applicable to me."[7]

Confessing What God Already Knows

What could be lovelier or more hopeful than the simple fact that you and I and David and the rest are invited by this psalm (and all of Scripture really) to make this very ask for mercy? Hidden beneath it is the humble assumption that God is listening, that God cares. The ask trusts in mercy, hopes for mercy, and even dares to expect mercy! Never presuming upon God, we ask, sensing God almost permits us to presume upon God, as the prodigal son returning home presumed his father would welcome him back.

How odd to confess, to ask, to turn yourself in to God, since God already knows. Lauren Winner illustrates the situation:

God already knows my real self, better than I will ever know it. The intimacy that follows my petitions is made possible not by

God's new knowledge of me but by my new availability to God. Consider a mundane analogy: My best friend finally tells me about the infatuation she has been nursing for two months. Of course, I spotted the infatuation myself seven weeks before. Still, our friendship deepens, not because I have learned anything new, but because in being willing to tell me about the crush, my friend has become more available to me.[8]

Thinking further about friendship: the early Methodists met in small groups weekly, opening the conversation with the question, "What sins have you committed since we were last together?" Oh my. I've invited groups in my churches to try this. No takers thus far. But Psalm 51 would have been prayed in front of others, along with others. It's accountability. And it's a profound kind of love for one another. Bonhoeffer, in a setting where his fellow pastors did this Methodist thing, noticed that "in confession there takes place a breakthrough to community. Sin wants to be alone with people. It takes them away from community. The more lonely people become, the more destructive the power of sin over them. The more deeply they become entangled in it, the more unholy is their loneliness."[9] Confessing sins to one another breaks the loneliness and breaks the power of sin over us.

Does posture matter in confession? You might kneel, bow your head, and close your eyes not out of shame or subservience but as a physical embodiment of coming defenseless before God. The way to your heart and your mind is through your body. Frederick Buechner's image moves me—that we live our lives like a clenched fist, which can work, fight, and hang on to things; but the clenched fist can never accept the helping hand. Do we open our palms to receive mercy?

Notice also the psalm speaks of transgressions—plural. We can never think, *I've just made this one mistake, so I'll confess it now.* Or, *It's not that I've made five booboos since I last prayed (although that's likely an underestimate).* Spurgeon is leading us somewhere when he writes, "Our God hath multitude of mercies. If our sins be in number as the hairs of our head, God's mercies are as the stars of heaven."[10] David's one act is a multifaceted, complex act (again, violating six of the Ten Commandments). And that one episode is symptomatic of a profoundly disordered self with all manner of waywardness, lots of brokenness, habits forged over a lifetime, resulting in the kind of person who could do what David did. Don't we discover in ourselves a complicated web of habits that have woven around and into us over a long time? We ask God to blot out our transgressions.

These transgressions linger, don't they, like a discoloring, a stain, a residue—even when they are past, confessed, and forgiven. Psalm 51 asks God to "blot out" (vv. 1, 9), then "wash me" and "cleanse me" (v. 2)—and down in verse 7, "purge me." We understand all too well how missteps and foolish decisions have their lasting consequences—for others as well as inside your own head and heart. Some toxic spills need to be cleaned up. Forgiveness isn't merely getting out of punishment. There's a healing, a cleaning that's needed—and actually happens even in the act of confessing.

Israelites understood "Purge me with hyssop," having witnessed the priest waving the fronds of a shrub dipped in water or blood, the mercy made tangible. "Wash me, and I will be whiter than snow" (v. 7), a line commemorated in the hymn "Have Thine Own Way, Lord." Modern revisions of the hymnal have edited out the "Whiter than snow, Lord, wash me just now,"[11] given the bad habit of white people, thinking of whiteness as superior, and the ways people of color have been disenfranchised and discriminated against. The psalm was first written and chanted by people of color, who had struggled to get stains out of white fabrics. Think red wine or blood on your white shirt, or the lovely artwork my two-year-old daughter scribbled on our new couch with a red ink pen.

God laughs as such impossible-to-remove stains are lifted. And the desire to be clean? I feel it keenly, and I hope and pray you do as well. I love C. S. Lewis's rationale for purgatory:

> Our souls *demand* Purgatory, don't they? Would it not break the heart if God said to us, "It is true, my son, that your breath smells and your rags drop with mud and slime, but we are charitable here and no one will upbraid you with these things, nor draw away from you. Enter into the joy"? Should we not reply, "With submission, sir, and if there is no objection, I'd rather be cleaned first."[12]

And maybe, just maybe, God's rescue and cleanup operation isn't limited to the sinner but behind the scenes is as or more effective for those painfully damaged by the sinner. God, after all, is bringing about a whole new creation.

Grieving God's Heart

Verse 3 might give us pause: "I know my transgressions." But do we? The sneakiest aspect of sin is the way we mistake good for bad and bad for good, how we paste God on the outside of what is mere personal preference. I'm mortified, yet weirdly relieved, to consider that we all (embarrassingly but inevitably) have blind spots. Plantation owners and their wives kept journals and wrote letters revealing their prayers, such as "Lord, show me how severely to punish my slave," or "Lord, should I purchase two more slaves?"—utterly blind to the brutal truth that the God to whom they prayed wished them to free those slaves. What are my blind spots? And can I trust God's mercy, not just to forgive, but to reveal, and then heal?

We can be sure, and grateful for it, that God has no blind spots. God sees all—which could feel like a threat, a helicopter God snooping into our dark corners. But this is our comfort and hope. God sees. God knows. David thought he could cover up his wickedness. But God saw. Stricken and embarrassed by what God sees, we come to realize that this is the love. This is the hope for healing.

Verse 4 is worth pulling apart for close inspection. The psalmist confesses to have "done that which is evil in thy sight." So many saints and martyrs have done what was good in God's sight but were regarded as evil or threatening in a world out of sync with God and have paid the price. God's sight? Spiritual growth is about realizing we live our lives on a stage with God as audience. God's cheering us on! But God notices when we veer off script, when we stumble, even if nobody else really notices. Again, so much mercy in this.

So then we may be perplexed, but then become delighted, that the psalmist confesses, "Against thee, thee only, have I sinned" (v. 4). Well, David and the rest of us have sinned not only against God but the others we've hurt. David might prefer to think it's only God from whom he needs to seek forgiveness. Did Bathsheba ever forgive him? Uriah could never forgive him. Could Uriah's family?

And yet to focus our deepest sense of contrition on God might bring healing and a holier future. When we hurt others, we grieve God. The closer you grow to God, the more it grieves you to grieve

God's heart. So instead of asking, How do I get off the hook or out of trouble? I can ask, How could I treat God this way? How could I treat those God loves this way? I love the Bidding Prayer in *Lessons and Carols*: "Because this of all things would rejoice his heart, let us at this time remember in his name the poor and helpless... and all those who know not the Lord Jesus, or who love him not, or who by sin have grieved his heart of love."[13] Want to know how special you are? And how special others are? You have the capacity to rejoice God's heart and to grieve God's heart.

Original Sin

Psalm 51 has left many modern people miffed in that it has provided fodder for theologians over the centuries to endorse or even prove the doctrine of original sin. "Behold, I was brought forth in iniquity, and in sin did my mother conceive me" (v. 5). Mind you, the Bible celebrates life in the womb and loving families that conceive new life. "Sons are a heritage from the LORD" (Psalm 127:3). "You knit me together in my mother's womb" (Psalm 139:13). Psalms, after all, are not dogmatic decrees but outbursts of despair or praise. Scrambling to find the words, this psalmist feels his whole life has been a mess; he, like us, is "prone to wander" (see Psalm 119). It's not as if he was all good and slipped once. In this dark season, his whole life feels like one huge slip. I am a sinner constitutionally.

Medieval theologians grasped after the idea that sin was passed on via conjugal relations—but we need not conclude as they did that sin is like a strand of DNA passed on biologically. The heart of "original sin" is the unavoidable truth that we all sin; we are all mired in a sinkhole not of our own devising but into which we heartily plunge. Young children aren't exactly generous or holy. Mark Twain was right: "I don't see why Adam and Eve get so much credit. I could have done just as well as they did." Or we can laugh at ourselves when we hear Lancelot boast early in the musical *Camelot*, "Had I been made the partner of Eve, we'd be in Eden still"—only to find himself in bed with Guinevere all too soon. We offer God not a one-off sin but a broken self, one we all share, always.

Create in Me a Clean Heart

Earlier, we explored the way the commandments are themselves mercy, especially the way Jesus seemed to be reaching into the marrow of each person listening (us included!) so we could realize Psalm 51:6 birthed in us: "Thou desirest truth in the inward being; therefore teach me wisdom in my secret heart." The unexpected surprise of our psalm, though, shows up in verses 8 and 12: "Fill me with joy and gladness," and "Restore to me the joy of thy salvation." The sorrowful confession of sin, wrestling with the ways we've grieved God's heart: How could this be the occasion for joy? Joy, we must realize, isn't being happy or feeling better. Joy is a sustained sense of the goodness of God's presence, the relief of not being defined by outward circumstances, the inner delight in God's love even in the thick of any and all kinds of suffering.

The crux of the whole psalm, and the only hope we have, is plain to see in verse 10: "Create in me a clean heart, O God." This is not a self-help manual. It's not about trying a little harder to be a little better. Create! Only God can "create," the Hebrew verb *bara'* was never used of anything any human being does. If God could create a universe, God can craft a whole new heart in you. Jeremiah 31:33 dreamed of a day when God's law didn't have to be learned but would be written directly into the heart. And Paul spoke of our life in Christ as, not people who are 37 percent better than others, but a "new creation" (2 Corinthians 5:17). Since God brought order out of chaos in Genesis 1, we can trust God to do something as transformative in me, in you, even in humanity.

Once we begin to live with the newly created heart, once we understand the mercy, we have a responsibility to tell our story to others. We can't help but tell, so marvelous is our joy! The psalm promises God just this: "Then I will teach....O Lord, open thou my lips" (Psalm 51:13, 15). Testimony is God's best way to reach into the heart of the skeptic, the doubter, and the one who believes he is abandoned by God. Testimony builds community. You narrate what unfolded, how surprised you've been by God.

This, after all, is the sacrifice God desires. Obviously God prescribed all those sacrifices so we'd live into the truth that it all really belongs to God and that if it costs you dearly to hurt somebody, you'll think twice next time before hurting somebody. But sacrifice can feel like buying your way into God's good graces instead of being welcomed freely. God is looking for a dismantled self, a broken openness. You might need to divest yourself of some of what you cling to that distances you from God. It's not less than sacrifice, but a full-bodied, full-souled sacrifice that frees you to be embraced by the mercy. "Present your bodies as a living sacrifice, holy and acceptable to God, which is your spiritual worship. Do not be conformed to this world but be transformed" (Romans 12:1-2).

4
Psalm 73

Hope:
For Me It Is Good to Be Near God

4

Psalm 73

Hope: For Me It Is Good to Be Near God

In the introduction, I shared my best Psalms story—of reading one in the morning and the next one in the evening as I'd stop by my friend Thaniel's hospital room as I came and went from the divinity school each day. Engaged in a titanic, exhausting battle against cystic fibrosis, she'd asked me to do so on the very day my doctoral professor Roland Murphy (who'd not spoken with Thaniel) declared that I should read a psalm in the morning and another in the evening.

Thaniel and I did not make it as far as Psalm 73. The morning after the night she'd died, I felt dazed, almost concussed walking the same hallway but with no point in stopping. I had barely entered the divinity school when, by a stroke of luck or by God's merciful habit of bringing his beloved ones together by "coincidence," I bumped into none other than Father Murphy. I choked up as I muttered, "Thaniel died." He wrapped his long arm over my slumped shoulders and said, gently and firmly, "She's with God."

In his class the day before, we'd been digging deeply into Psalm 73 and the hard, healing surgery it can do to your soul, especially regarding the suffering of God's beloved ones and what really happens after death. And so, Psalm 73 will probably always be my answer to the question, What is your favorite psalm?

Psalm 73 was Jewish philosopher Martin Buber's favorite too. He asked that verses 23 and 24 be inscribed on his tombstone. Charles Wesley composed the very last of his sixty-five hundred hymns on his deathbed, inspired by Psalm 73, his favorite. Walter Brueggemann rightly said, "This psalm is an act of faith" (an insightful way to think of a psalm), and, "It is a mighty engagement with God, a struggle against God, and a wondrous communion with God."[1] Perhaps best of all, Spurgeon called this psalm "the narrative of a great soul-battle, a spiritual Marathon."[2] Walk with me through this great text, if you're ready for what you'll someday have to be ready for: a wrestling with God and who God really is, a contest over who you really are and why you're here, and some clues and possibilities about life being more than just this life and what anything beyond might look like.

Surely God Is Good

And so we begin where the psalm begins: "Surely God is good to Israel, to those who are pure in heart" (NIV). It's a proverbial saying, a memorizable verse that seems self-evident, chock full of truth, something your grandmother cross-stitched and framed above her hearth or one that would appear as a truthy saying on a poster or in a social media meme. Surely God's job is to be good to us, especially if we are good. God is good. All the time! But surely to the upright, the pure in heart, the believers, and the good people.

Don't scurry too quickly past that first word, *surely*. Why not just leave it off and declare "God is good to Israel, to those who are upright"? Doth that word protest too much? *Surely* invites you to ask, Are you sure? Doesn't it leave the door open just a crack, leaving us some wiggle room? Isn't there a hidden question tucked inside? *Surely* is why you bother to read on. There's space already for anybody who harbors a few suspicions that "God is good to the pure in heart" might not always hold. *Surely*? Is it like smiling and saying "I'm fine" when you're hiding the fact that you aren't? Is it singing "I believe" when in your gut you might or might not really?

What a healing gift the psalmist offers next: "But as for me…" (Psalm 73:2). Think of the courage it takes to be honest enough, vulnerable enough, or maybe desperate enough to open up to those who are very sure (or sure seem to be sure) that God is good to the pure in heart! But you just have to tell somebody. Maybe by blurting it out, you can finally own it for yourself. And you hope that if you risk a little candor, you might get repaid with somebody else's candor. There's got to be somebody grinning to "God is good to the upright, / to those who are pure in heart" (Psalm 73:1) who's also a mess inside. You might just make a friend, a real friend. You need one right now.

Even the little word "but." There's always a "but," isn't there? Naaman "was a mighty man of valor, *but* he was a leper" (2 Kings 5:1, emphasis added). There was a man who had two sons, *but* one of them squandered it all in a foreign land (Luke 15). I love my husband, but

I think he drinks too much. I go to church and pray all the time, but God doesn't answer. What is your "but"?

The psalmist's "but" is intriguing and far from unusual. "But as for me, my feet had almost stumbled, / my steps had well nigh slipped" (Psalm 73:2). You are walking along with a simple faith, but then—oops—you slip. You stumble. You fall down. And in the life of faith, stumbling surprises you, and it hurts. And what do you do next? Pick yourself up, dust yourself off, and keep moving?

Notice the little word *almost*. Not down yet, still moving along with this simple faith. But gee, it's tough going here! The path isn't so solid anymore. And if he "almost" stumbled, we're safe to assume he didn't finally fall into some abyss but found his way. Did he ask some hard questions (like, Is God really good to the pure in heart? or, Is there really a good God?) but then grit his teeth and march onward? After all, he'd been told not to ask questions, that there's shame in wondering about God.

Or (and this is the hope in his "almost") did he pull the whole thing apart? God? is good? to the pure in heart? Can we discern how, after struggling mightily and praying intently, he managed to stitch it all back together—maybe like a repaired pair of britches that aren't as pretty as new ones but are sturdier for the patching and fresh threads holding it tightly?

Envying the Arrogant

What nearly made him stumble? "For I was envious of the arrogant, / when I saw the prosperity of the wicked" (Psalm 73:3). Arrogance. An unpleasant trait, the antithesis of holy humility; the puffed-up think they're better than others. And can you feel the psalmist feeling the blunt edge of the arrogance of people he knows—or wishes he knew? They look down not just on others but on him? "I saw the prosperity of the wicked." It's safe to assume our psalmist was poor, with zero prosperity. "The prosperity of the wicked"! Well, they must be wicked to have hoarded so much; their haughty looks are a dead giveaway of wickedness underneath.

There's more. "For they have no pangs; / their bodies are sound and sleek" (v. 4). Could it be that they could afford better medical care, they were sheltered from the elements, and they had access to oils, spas, trainers, and beauticians? And you can bet the psalmist had pangs, and his body was unsound and rickety, marked by years of poverty or illness. "They are not in trouble" (as they can always maneuver or pay their way out of it) "as other men" (like the psalmist!) "are; / they are not stricken like other men" (v. 5). Stricken? Down in verse 14, the psalmist is explicit: "All the day long I have been stricken." Stricken with…what? We can't know, but it's a strong word. He's the victim of something awful and constant.

"Pride is their necklace; / violence covers them as a garment" (v. 6). Wearing shiny jewels (which the psalmist couldn't afford) around their necks; metaphorically, it's their pride they wear. Were they violent? Did they beat their servants or competitors in business? Were they tax collectors who broke your knees if you failed to pay up?

This psalmist may be a sick, poor nobody, but he has rhetorical flair. "Their eyes swell out with fatness, / their hearts overflow with follies" (v. 7). You can picture the wide-eyed, arrogant ones who are…full of it? "They set their mouths against the heavens, / and their tongue struts through the earth" (v. 9). The cocky, the highfalutin can't stop chattering about how great they are, full of mockery and conceit. Their pompous words are blathering evidence of the evil within bearing witness against itself.

Yet, "people turn and praise them" (v. 10). Indeed. Don't we see people fawning over the wrong people? Not the humble and holy and not the sufferers and the ostracized—the ones God asks us to turn toward. No, people avert their gaze but can't restrain their giddy admiration of the vapid, destructive ones. For they are what fallen humanity always craves: "These are the wicked; / always at ease, they increase in riches" (v. 12). Once again, the Seven Deadly Sins—which the church has warned us about for centuries: greed, sloth, pride, envy, lust, wrath, and gluttony—have come to be prized as the good life in America.

It's the Contrasts

Fascinating. The psalmist's satirical sizing up of those arrogant rich who were—who? His neighbors? His employers? People who tossed a few coins his way for his wares? Those whose houses he cleaned? His critique is spot-on and theologically insightful! But how artfully he tells his own story while carping at them. So it's not just his own suffering, which would be bad enough. It's the comparison, the many comparisons—or we should say contrasts.

It's always that way. If you're alone, it's the people with happy families that make you feel worse. If you're chronically ill, it's the healthy, active ones who rub it in. If you're scrapping to pay your bills, it's the spendthrifts doling it all over the place who make you crazy. If you're struggling to accept your own infertility, it pierces you to sit in church watching cascades of toddlers rampaging the hallways. If you have dark doubts about God, it's tough to be in the company of the serene, grinning, and cocksure spiritual ones.

It's not so bad—or is it worse?—when those who prosper, who are well thought of, are the righteous! Why are the others like me doing so well while I'm barely surviving? What's the point of it all?

The fact that the contrasts bug you itself bugs you, and you feel guilt for resenting others. Piling on! Sometimes, we who are comfy or even faithful *do* the piling on. We talk too loosely about God's blessings, which we think are "things," like a nice house, a good job, or even our health. But we always say these things within earshot of somebody who is chronically ill, who's lost everything, or who's had it taken away. The idea that the good are rewarded and the wicked are punished is absurd to thinking people. Many who are rich and healthy are not so holy; otherwise, you could peer in the windows of the biggest houses and find there champions of morality and piety. Don't we all know people who are extraordinarily good and holy but who suffer awfully?

Why Do Bad Things Happen?

So Psalm 73 is batting around the problem of why there is suffering if God is good. For years, people would ask me, "Why do bad things happen to good people?" I'd start by trying to fix their question. Why should bad things happen to bad people? Even more simply, Why do bad things happen? And who are we to say we're the good ones? And yet, the psalmist wonders. He evaluates, in retrospect, his lifetime spent in striving to be holy, in avoiding sin, in making his sacrifices, his diligence in prayer and worship, and in doing what he could for others. "All in vain have I kept my heart clean / and washed my hands in innocence" (v. 13). Heartbreaking words.

Can you feel his wrenching regret? Have you ever wondered if being a churchgoer, refraining from the fun, keeping your vows, or spending extended time in prayer haven't just been ineffective but a regrettable waste of time? Shouldn't all that effort have somehow made everything turn out better? Derek Kidner reads verse 13's "All in vain..." as self-centered.[3] But this psalmist is human, and God wants to use his feelings to make space for and welcome lovingly any and everybody who's ever felt this way.

The "But as for me" in verse 2 was not silenced, and we needn't silence sufferers with our pithy silliness. As some might say, "God's in control"—but with wars, starvation, abuse, and even children suffering from cancer or homelessness, God is either lousy at being in control or is a monster. "God won't give you more than you can handle," they say—but does God measure your "handle-ability" and then dole out only slightly fewer agonies? I was in the pew next to a dear friend at her husband's funeral when the pastor assured us that "he's in a better place"—prompting her to growl, "I wanted him here." C. S. Lewis delivered very popular lectures on *The Problem of Pain*, suggesting that sufferings are God's "hammer blows" to awaken and to discipline us: "God whispers to us in our pleasures, speaks in our conscience, but shouts in our pains: it is His megaphone to rouse a deaf world."[4] But then his wife Joy died too young from cancer, and he never again spoke of hammer blows or megaphones.

After Joy's death, Lewis wrote that he not only hated being alone but also wished people who'd visit would talk to one another but not to him. In the face of suffering, you can be present, and it's best while present simply to be silent. I learned this on the evening the doctor had delivered the knee-buckling news to Thaniel that she would not recover, that there was no hope. Thaniel told me. Her mom was in the room, her back to me as she stared out the window into the dark. Grieving and fumbling around—I mean, I was a pastor, at least a pastor-in-training—I thought I should say something. "Mrs. Armistead, would you like for me to pray?" Her bitter response, without turning from the dark window, put me in my place: "Pray if you want. Nobody's listening."

We are either skimming or reading our Bibles selectively if we think there are pat answers to suffering in there somewhere. So many psalms, the prophet Jeremiah, pitiable Job, and the Lord Jesus himself on the cross cry out in exasperation at God, or about God, questioning in utter despair, Why?

I tried my hand at correcting some of the absurd and downright harmful answers to Why? in my book *The Will of God*. A friend's husband was killed in a plane crash. She asked why God took him. Not in that moment but years later, I reflected with her that when the Wright brothers made that first flight at Kitty Hawk, humanity made a bargain. For the thrill, speed, and convenience of flight, we'll accept the risk and reality that human error or the weather or a bird strike will once in a while take a plane and our loved ones down. God doesn't swat planes from the air. A neighbor of mine was shot and killed. God didn't kill him; a sinful, addicted criminal did that. A fellow pastor's daughter was killed—in church—by a tornado. God didn't blow the church down. Wind and storms happen, and they are probably worse because of the toxins we humans have spread around God's good earth.

Psalm 73 doesn't simplistically answer these "why" questions. The arrogant prosper and strut. The faithful man is poor and stricken. "Why" fades into unimportance given the journey this psalmist makes and the story he shares with us in the balance of the psalm. We're at the turning point in the plot. Everything is about to change. Verse 16 opens with the fateful word we've navigated earlier: "but." The first "but" begged to differ from the naive religion that clings to the notion that God blesses the good people, rewarding them for the favors they've done God. "But as for me" led us into a vivid sample of why that version of what God is about just doesn't work.

Now, we see another "but." The God who doesn't dole out favors for those who do the right thing, who show up at church and stick around with nice people doing nice things, this God has a very different and surprising "but" for the psalmist. Yet it's not one that God thunders down triumphantly from on high. This "but" emerges from the psalmist's own experience. So let's get ready to change our minds, as the psalmist changed his own mind.

Reorientation in the Sanctuary

Brueggemann provides us with a grid for understanding how Psalms work and how they move us from where we've been to where we're hopefully going: they *disorient* us, and then, they *reorient* us. The Seventy-Third Psalm rattles the conventional wisdom (God is good to the pure in heart) until it comes unhinged. Its pieces, God, experience, your heart, goodness, and pain are lying on the floor, waiting for the psalmist to put Humpty back together again, but in a fresh, sturdier, more hopeful shape.

And for this psalmist, the turning point, the major twist in its plot, comes in verse 17: "I went into the sanctuary of God." The Jerusalem temple was an architectural marvel, the most magnificent building (actually, the most magnificent humanly crafted thing!) any Israelite had ever seen, massive, with torches burning, the sun gleaming through windows onto bronze-coated walls and pillars, exotic draperies hanging, and the intoxicating smell of incense. During the high festivals, our psalmist would have heard trumpets blaring, cymbals clashing, and the crowds chanting. But now he was overwhelmed by the astonishing hush, the utter silence of such a place. "Be still, and know that I am God" (Psalm 46:10) probably came to mind and stilled his anxious soul.

What did the Israelites think would happen in this sacred place, God's own house? They came of course seeking blessing and mercy but often got far more. Isaiah also "went into the sanctuary of God," and the place, which seemed so solid, morphed into life: cherubim and seraphim flying and singing. Over the centuries, God's people have crept quietly into sanctuaries of every size and shape, looking for...you name it. Do we ever sense the place is mystically alive, even on fire, with the presence of God? Annie Dillard suggested that we wear not flowery bonnets to church but crash helmets.[5]

A poignant moment in Jan Karon's novel *At Home in Mitford*: Father Tim slips into his little chapel and notices a man in the pew praying, his voice rising until he almost shouts, "If you're up there, prove it! Show me!...Are...you...up...there?" Father Tim slides in beside the man and says, "I believe the question you may want to ask is not, 'Are you up there?' but 'Are you down here?'"[6]

I happened upon a homeless woman who'd found her way to the kneeling rail of my sanctuary one night. Her praying, too, became audible: "I need some help down here!" A Bible study class meeting down the hall took her in and befriended her for years, getting her and her kids back on their feet.

Even people who don't believe in or think twice about God are blessed in sanctuaries by that very God they don't believe in. I know people in big cities who slip into a quiet sanctuary on a weekday afternoon and find solace. God's that good. God works in the sanctuary.

He Came to Himself

Our psalmist went into the sanctuary. Why? He might have entertained the idea of abandoning his faith, but he couldn't quite let go. In the dark void of his soul, he really had no place left to turn. In this sacred space, he anticipated what Jesus would speak of in his very best story—the one about the prodigal son, mired in a pigsty far from home: "He came to himself" (Luke 15:17). God, who of course dwelled everywhere but cherished that temple as something of a home base, noticed the psalmist walking through the door. And God smiled the way the father in Jesus's story smiled when the prodigal appeared on the horizon. God smiled the way an old grandmother in a nursing home smiles after watching the door for so very long and then becomes giddy with delight because he's come home. What does that grandmother want? The same thing God wants. She isn't hoping he'll bring ice cream or a new laptop or anything. She just wants him to come, to be with her, to see his face, and to hear his voice—his presence.

And that is what God wants from us. God wants us to show up, simply to be there, and to be present. And God not only wants that from us. God wants that for us. Here's the climax of our psalm, and in fact it's also the climax of my life and yours: "God is good to the...pure in heart" (v. 1). The "good" that God gives isn't this or that tangible reward; the "good" isn't even health or wealth. No, God is the good, the one whose love never fails, the one who shows up (causing us to realize that God never left). What God gives is God's own self. Listen to the transparent passion and simple eloquence of the psalmist, beginning with his newly discovered "But as for me," expanded (since it's even more wonderful now) to "Nevertheless."

> Nevertheless I am continually with thee;
> > thou dost hold my right hand....
> > And there is nothing upon earth that I desire besides thee.
> My flesh and my heart may fail,
> > but God is the strength of my heart and my
> > portion for ever....
>
> But for me it is good to be near God.
> > (Psalm 73:23, 25-26, 28)

For the God who is present, always, even if God seems far away to us, the "good" God offers and lavishly supplies is nearness, intimacy.

God Came to Be Near Us

It's fascinating how this psalm anticipates (without a hint of predicting!) what God would ultimately do to be near us. God became small, a wee one in the womb of Mary, born like the rest of us in the flesh, wanting what all infants want: some tenderness and some peaceful care. And as that infant, Jesus offered what all infants offer us: the chance to be gentle, to coo, to be in awe, and to sigh—and smile. No deals are made. No conversation happens. It's just the tenderest, most fulfilling love imaginable: just being in the presence of a child. No wonder God thought the best possible nickname for Jesus would be Immanuel—God with us, God near us. God is good. For me, it is good to be near God. God didn't promise to make you healthy or wealthy. God did promise always to be with us. God came to be near us, which was good for God and good for us.

And so, we've not only redefined "good." We also have shed a few illusions about "God." The true God is not the great cashier in the sky who rewards our goodness. God isn't the weaver of an invisible spell of protection around us. God is love; God is the one who was truly good but came down and suffered a terrible, painful, young death while Jesus's friends ran for shelter. God looks down on our suffering and does not say, "It is my will." Instead, God takes our suffering onto the divine heart; God engages in stunning solidarity with us in our "But as for me…"

God is near, whether we feel it or not, because God promised. Jesus found himself alone in the wilderness with the devil trying to get his claws into him, when Jesus was gradually abandoned by his friends who knew him best, when Jesus prayed until sweat-like drops of blood bobbed on his brow, and when Jesus cried out in an eerie darkness that settled in the middle of the day, "My God, my God, why hast thou forsaken me?" (Matthew 27:46; Mark 15:34). We trust the undeniable fact of God's presence, not our feelings about God's presence or apparent lack thereof. Could it even be that if you feel far from God, God is even closer than you could ever expect? Could it be that God's desire to be "near" us is the impulse behind Jesus serving bread and wine to his disciples—and to us—saying, "This is my body"? When you take that holy, mystical bread, you hold Jesus very close, then closer, then right into your mouth and your body. How much closer could you get than Jesus down inside you, becoming a part of you?

If God's good is God's own self, then a "pure heart" can't mean merely doing nice things or avoiding what's naughty. What comes out of the heart? Love. The pure in heart love. The pure heart is pure as it is loved. The pure heart simply loves. The pure heart loves God and is loved by the pure heart of God. God is good and near to the pure in heart.

Eternal Life?

I was jolted to my core when Father Murphy explained how the Old Testament knows nothing about resurrection or eternal life. When you die, you're dead. What? But read carefully, and you'll see: the Old Testament is obsessed with what God is doing in this world and exhibits no abiding interest in or hope for life after death.

The question to ponder is this: Without life after death, would you behave better or worse now? Old Testament people would answer "better" since this life is all you've got to leave your mark, your legacy. We might also ask if the dangling carrot of eternal life sets you up to be good only for your own benefit. A young man, emerging from lifelong atheism, asked me if he could be a Christian and not believe in eternal life. Caught off guard, I said, "Yes—but why do you ask?" He replied that he wanted to be a Christian simply because it was true and good, whether he got any benefit out of it or not. I loved his thought process! But I asked him, "So, what if when you die, God still surprises you with eternal life?" He said that would be okay.

From his confinement in a Nazi prison cell, Dietrich Bonhoeffer wrote to a friend that he was reading more and more of the Old Testament—suggesting that "it is only when one loves life and the earth so much that without them everything seems to be over that one may believe in the resurrection and a new world."[7] Our psalmist loved life and the earth. But when he came to himself, he discovered his one true love: his love for God, so much so that without it, everything seemed to be over. And so we can now make sense of his impassioned prayer:

> *I am continually with thee . . .*
> *Whom have I in heaven but thee?*
>> *And there is nothing upon earth that I desire besides thee.*
> *My flesh and my heart may fail,*
>> *but God is the strength of my heart and my portion for ever.*
>>> *(Psalm 73:23, 25-26)*

Forever? In these words, do we overhear a tentative venture into the possibility of eternal life? He loves God so much he would grieve death's breaking of the bond—like all of our loves. And in that love, is he intuiting that God's love for him is so powerful that God does not wish for it to end either? And couldn't that be the healthiest, most robust, and frankly beautiful sense of what eternal life is? Not golden streets or angel's wings, but a "love that wilt not let me go," forever with "Jesus, lover of my soul" (to pick up on hymns we sing). And if this is eternal life, then life today, however daunting, partakes already of that undying love? We pray, then, simpler prayers, like "Here I am, Lord; here you are; here we are together."[8]

Another inspired hint in this psalmist's heart and words peeks out in verse 24's baffling "and afterward thou wilt receive me to glory." Sounds like heaven, but nowhere else in the Bible is heaven spoken of this way! "Afterward" (the Hebrew is much debated by scholars) seems to mean "later" or "toward," and "glory" is most likely an adverb, "gloriously." Our psalmist, wanting the love with God never to end, yet still mired in being poor and stricken, trusts this God, moving forward, to receive him gloriously. I firmly believe if we could go back and interview him and ask, "What on earth did you mean by that?" he'd say, "Not sure. It just came into my head, but I believe it came there from God, and it's all about hope."

Hope is ultimately the theme of this great psalm. Hope isn't figuring things will get better tomorrow. That's optimism, which depends on your attitude and sunny outcomes. Hope is much better than optimism. Hope does not demand a particular outcome. Hope is about trusting God will be there. Hope is even ready for the worst that might come.

Other Lingering Things

I find myself wishing the psalmist had kept verses 18-20 to himself—his seeming delight that the arrogant he'd complained about and suffered under will slip, fall to ruin, and be destroyed, "swept away utterly by terrors." We are never swift to learn to love those who have afflicted us. I would hope that, over the years, our psalmist might come to realize that they too are loved by the God who only wants to be near them too and that their only hope is the same as his—in discovering God's nearness. Of course, their follies are foolishness and will not last into the eternity our psalmist is beginning to visualize.

There's something we skipped, but now we can backtrack and understand. In verse 15, we read the enigmatic "If I had said, 'I will speak thus'" (that is, in the wake of suffering, and mired in envious comparison with those less holy, we declare either that God proved to be a dud or that a life of prayer, holiness, and service was a colossal waste of time), "I would have been untrue to the generation of / thy children." I had to puzzle over this for a long time. Fortunately, I had Father Murphy's wisdom to guide me.

The psalmist learned it was "good to be near God" largely because of "the generation of thy children" (v. 15)—the body of believers. John Goldingay's translation helps: "I would have broken faith with the circle of your children."⁹ The psalmist's change of heart resulted from sanctuary and community. We help one another to believe, to survive dark days, and to cling to God when God seems absent. Invisibly but surely, even the saints who have died hover in the sanctuary and envelop us with love, faith, and power. One moment, we feel alone and desolate; but in the sanctuary, we are enveloped in much love, God's love, the church's love, and we nod, recognizing the only good that matters—and it is enough: "As for me, it is good to be near God."

And we cry out to God in our misery, in the company of others, in God's church across town, in other countries, and in other times. Might our outcries to God be tempered or calmed down a bit and find themselves in good company if we recall the cries of our grandparents during the Great Depression or World Wars I and II, or those of persecuted Christians in communist or fascist regimes? Could any of us be lazy Bible students when we think of those who were executed for smuggling Bibles? Saints and martyrs pray with us, and we are reminded to try to be true to them when we cry out—which may lead us, with the psalmist, in some embarrassment, to admit, "When my soul was embittered...I was stupid and ignorant" (vv. 21-22).

Can I be true to my friend Thaniel in my praying? When I learned she would not leave the hospital alive, I was shattered. But Thaniel was concerned for *me*. She comforted me. *She* believed and trusted in God when I struggled to do so in the light of *her* suffering!—and I was healthy! Our titanic questions about God's goodness and who prospers are in some small but so very lovely measure answered by the Thaniels God gifts us with. They comfort us in their suffering and believe when we doubt. I am moved when I visit various Holocaust memorials, and I see prayer shawls, haunting reminders that, in the ghettos and concentration camps of World War II, Jews still gathered every day, donned those shawls, and spoke and chanted their praises to their God. For them, as for me, it was and is good to be near God.

5
Psalm 90

Time:
Living with
Moses

5

Psalm 90

Time: Living with Moses

Psalm 90 has occupied more hours of my life than any other—by far. When I turned in my doctoral dissertation at Duke, I inserted a joke title page: "More Than You'd Ever Want to Know about Psalm 90." For three years, I had read and analyzed everything everybody had ever said about this psalm: modern-day scholars and the Church Fathers of ancient times; Martin Luther, John Calvin, Augustine, and dozens of medieval theologians; and sermons by famous and obscure preachers, musings by poets and diarists, and even the hymns of Isaac Watts and Charles Wesley. Upon completion, I probably had amassed in my brain more knowledge about this psalm than anyone who'd ever lived.

But don't take that as a brag. In my final analysis, I was left with unresolved quandaries, more baffled than when I'd begun, awestruck by the mystery and majesty of this small sample of the human words to God become the Word of God we know as the Psalms. I felt a bit embarrassed and defeated when I was done.

But my inability to master a single psalm in three years, my bowing before the mystery of the Word, is as it should be. More moments in Scripture than we'd care to admit simply elude us. Why did God accept Abel's offering but not Cain's? Why did Nadab and Abihu have to die (Leviticus 10)?—which, if you're not familiar, has baffled all scholars! We can guess or make clever deductions. But the truth is, we do not know. And God does not wish for us to know. It's the not knowing that reminds us we're speaking now of God and mysteries beyond our capacities. Psalm 90 leads us, like a mountain guide, to a place where the air is thin, and you're glad not to tumble, your jaw drops in awe—and you can't explain it to your family once you're back down.

I chose Psalm 90 because I was working with Father Roland Murphy, America's greatest Psalms scholar, who doubled as America's greatest scholar of the Bible's Wisdom books: Job, Proverbs, and Ecclesiastes. Psalm 90 is often grouped together with a handful of others (32, 49, 111, and 128) dubbed "wisdom psalms," as they feel more like reflective ruminations than prayers. Plus, it was a psalm I'd read at the handful of graveside funerals I'd conducted as a very young pastor.

Decades later, the psalm took on a new, lovely life for me. My much-beloved mother-in-law, Jean, was turning eighty. I wanted to honor her with something extraordinary (and to pad my resume in the running for Son-in-Law of the Year). Knowing her to be a Bible scholar, I thought of Psalm 90:10, which suggestively speaks of being eighty years old!

Then, connecting other dots, I remembered admiring the beautiful folios of *The St. John's Bible*, those modern handwritten and artistically illuminated pages of Scripture—and that Psalm 90 was one of only five psalms featuring a beautiful, colorful folio page. I reached out to the publisher and ordered a sixteen-inch by twenty-three-inch print of the psalm and the art, had it framed (expensively, I'd add), and then presented it to her on her birthday. She, of course, was giddy with delight over this gift (and me?). After thanking me at length, she looked at me and said, "I guess when I die, you'll get this back for yourself." And so it came to pass. Today it hangs in my home office, a cherished reminder of her, of that moment, and of my long life with Psalm 90.

When I think of that gift, her life and death, and my own advancing years, I realize we are already into the heart of Psalm 90, with its themes of the passing of time, the transitory nature of even the best we have here, and inevitably, my passing and yours. How fitting, then, that this one psalm, and no other, bears the name of Moses. Mind you, scholars doubt—and for sound reasons—that Moses actually composed it. Even if he didn't, weren't those entrusted with compiling the Psalms into Scripture onto something when they attached his name to this one? It fits him like a glove.

Moses's Remarkable Life

Psalm 90 has everything we know about Moses etched all over it: themes of time, wilderness, wisdom, survival, and mortality. The very poetic image of God as a massive rock and refuge? Moses was the preeminent "Man of the Mountain" (as Zora Neale Hurston aptly named her lovely novel about him).

Let's recall Moses's very long, varied, and complex life. Born not in the best of times but in the very worst of times, Moses stepped onto the stage of history during the blinding hot days of Israel's enslavement in Egypt. The pharaoh—the most comfortable, powerful, and unquestioned man in the world, believed by his own people to be a god strutting across the earth—grew paranoid and hatched a laughably stupid idea to kill the baby boys, his future labor supply and potential fathers to even more babies and laborers. Moses must have been the best-behaved baby in history, so quiet his mother Jochebed could hide him away for three months (Exodus 2:2)! But his cries couldn't be hushed, just as those of God's people couldn't be silenced.

And so she cast her bread upon the waters, desperately parting with her beloved, hoping against hope, setting her hapless, helpless infant adrift in a basket on the Nile. Big sister Miriam kept a watchful eye. God too was watching behind the reedy banks. That basket floated (by chance? or by a divine nudging of the current) to Pharaoh's palace where (by chance? or by some little voice saying, "Go, now"?) one of Pharaoh's dozens of daughters happened (happened?) to have gone to bathe. She saw and had compassion and took him home. She was hardly noticed by Pharaoh, who had over a hundred children. In her father's house there were many mansions…

So Moses grew up in luxury, with the finest teachers and academic and military training. Visit the temples, palaces, and grand tombs of the pharaohs, and you blush over the exotic, impressive ambience of Moses's formative years. But he was still a Hebrew. Witnessing typical Egyptian brutality—an overseer punishing a slave—Moses was enraged enough, and virile enough, to kill the guy. Although he'd hidden the body in the sand, he realized the secret was out. So he went on the lam and fled to the Sinai desert—an exile, reduced to tending sheep just to survive. He fell in love with Zipporah and married.

All was well enough until, one day, not praying and certainly not seeking God's direction or even help, he saw something, and heard a voice, the first of many times in Scripture captured slyly by Elie Wiesel: "If an angel ever says, 'Be not afraid,' you'd better watch out. A big assignment is on the way."[1] Moses's assignment? To walk back into the corridors of power—his adopted father's domain!—and demand that the most powerful man on earth simply let his labor force walk away scot-free.

My first term paper in seminary was on this moment of Moses's encounter at the burning bush and his call. Digging around, I learned that this fits a common pattern in the Bible (and our lives). God surprises someone with a call, not based on a strong resume or profound spirituality. The one called is shocked, backpedals, explaining to God why it can't be—or why he won't go. Good reasons always: Moses can't speak; Isaiah isn't holy enough; Jeremiah is too young; Jonah thinks the Ninevites are too wicked to be saved; and Mary has never lain with a man. But God overrides every objection, looking not for ability but avail-ability.

A Long and Finally Frustrating Life

And so Moses goes. What a life! At home in the sumptuous palace, banished to a barren desert, and now back in the palace but as a wayward ingrate and enemy of the state. How dramatic was his contest with Pharaoh? How dramatic was that rescue of the Israelites by the sea? Yet Moses could never rest on his laurels or bask in his titanic victories. He right away—and for decades—had to lead hardheaded people who seemed hell-bent on going back to Egypt! Can you think of any leader who's ever experienced more relentless frustration than Moses?

Moses had his one bright shining moment too. On Mount Sinai, he didn't just receive the Ten Commandments, which alone may be the greatest single human achievement or honor ever. He spoke with God, with unparalleled intimacy. He asked to see God's glory. God, merciful to the one God favored, shielded him from what would blind or annihilate any of us and let him have a peek at God's back (Exodus 33). Moses's face, everybody noticed, glowed afterward. But was Paul right (2 Corinthians 3:7) when he suggested the glow faded as time passed?

Whew! Moses. That's a lot of living, ups and downs, valleys, and literal peaks. But you sense Moses wasn't entirely happy. He was riddled by some sadness, some existential weariness, discouragement, and melancholy he couldn't shake—reminding me of Qoheleth, the writer of the Wisdom book Ecclesiastes, who had it all, experienced it all, yet sighed and understood it was all vanity, vanity of vanities, nothing new under the sun.

And then, after his trials and thankless exertions for people who frankly didn't care for him very much, Moses died prematurely. That's hard to say of someone 120 years old! But he'd made it to his life's destination, the dream of all dreams, to the very brink of the Promised Land. He could see it from the peak of Mount Nebo. Just a few more days! But God—surely with tender, grieving compassion—told him he would die on that mountain, not down there in the land God had promised.

But why? Scholars and Sunday school teachers fish around to pinpoint the reason. Usually they say it's because, when seeking water, he struck the rock wrongly (Numbers 20). But God retaliates for one booboo, one in which Moses is trying to provide for his people? Is God the kind of God who doles out a sentence based on the worst thing you ever did (contrary to Bryan Stevenson's famous assertion that "each of us is more than the worst thing we've ever done"[2])? The not-very-religious thinker Franz Kafka got it right: Moses died because, like the rest of us, he was mortal.

The themes that ran through Moses's life like threads in a brilliant tapestry, time, mortality, frustration, sin, troubles, prayer, trust, God's elusiveness, God's presence, and hope against hope: all of these surface in Psalm 90. Let's look closely at the text, and these themes that never make it into light dinner conversation—yet are too important to leave on the back burner.

Time

Is there any text in all of Scripture that ponders the passing of time as eloquently as Psalm 90? Derek Kidner is right: "Only Isaiah 40 can compare with this psalm for its presentation of God's grandeur and eternity over against the frailty of man."[3] And isn't wisdom largely a reckoning with the passing of time? Wisdom's never glib about time and sometimes slips into a bit of a funk about the way time is in such a hurry. And then wisdom embraces the inevitability of time's steady march, knowing we only understand ourselves, God, and hope from the big perspective of time.

God made time. Time is God's great gift to us. God has time for us. Our times are in God's hands (Psalm 31:15). God embraces all time, all times, all at once, the way a child might hold a dandelion. God is beyond, yet in the thick of time, which gives us cause to trust: "O God, our help in ages past, our hope for years to come."

We have the possibility of "making the most of the time" (Ephesians 5:16). Time feels like a train whose brakes have failed, careening down a hill, faster and faster. How do we slow things down? The only way to slow things down is to slow down. The fantasy of American life, that you can jam time full and it will feel more full, is a deception. No wonder God built into our time what feels like a rule but is an actually treasured gift: the Sabbath, time for our often unacknowledged need to be still, and know that God is God (Psalm 46:10)—and that you aren't!

In God's perspective, "A thousand years in thy sight / are but as yesterday... / or as a watch in the night" (Psalm 90:4). I like the night-watch image. From the dark recesses of outer space, God is overseeing us and the world and time. Even a long life is too short, yet a wonder to behold. Or is it too long? Or is our waiting for God to show up and redeem things taking forever? Psalm 90 echoes dozens of others with an agonized pleading: "How long?"

I love the English translation "threescore and ten" (v. 10), instead of the simpler "seventy"—as if Lincoln were whispering in the psalmist's ear, heightening the marvel of the years. Then "fourscore"—a nearly impossible length of life in ancient times, although Moses exceeded that. But there's no glamour in living long, as the elderly know, bearing their aches and losses. "Their span is but toil and trouble" (v. 10), a phrase so spot-on that Shakespeare lifted it for *Macbeth*.

Our psalmist invites us to pray with him, "Teach us to number our days," as this yields "a heart of wisdom" (v. 12). Who knows the precise number? And if we knew (as John Irving's Owen Meany did in *A Prayer for Owen Meany* or the siblings in Chloe Benjamin's *The Immortalists*), we'd be haunted. Jesus told of a guy building ever-bigger barns, unable to count that today was his last day and the barns would matter not at all (Luke 12:16-21). This counting urges us to slow down and make each day count, not to rush; to be at peace, grateful, humbled, as if this day may be the last. It takes time to ponder. Mary pondered. Moses pondered. You too can be a ponderer, if you redeem the time God has given you.

Man of the Mountain

We associate Moses with the wilderness. Spurgeon's eloquence moves me: "Moses, in effect, says—wanderers though we be in the howling wilderness, yet we find a home in thee, even as our forefathers did when they came out of Ur...King's palaces have vanished beneath the crumbling hand of time."[4] Shelley's memorable poem "Ozymandias" sizes up the tumbled, crumbled statue of the great Pharaoh Rameses II, his arrogant sneer lying on the sand, nothing now but a "colossal Wreck." Did Moses know this Rameses? Was he (as many conclude) Moses's adoptive father? Moses surely had seen that colossal statue upright, before it was a wreck. Had the psalmist—maybe?—seen it? He'd have known of the eventual ruin of Egyptian power, as happens to worldly powers.

But Moses was defined less by the wilderness than by mountains. Not just any mountain but *the* mountain, Mount Sinai, where he spent weeks up there in the cold, amid the clouds, more intimate with God than anyone had ever been or would ever be again. Psalm 90:1:

"Lord, thou hast been our dwelling place," the Hebrew implying a large mountain with caves and crevices in which to hide or even live, a moving image of God. Many psalms employ a cluster of kindred terms. The LORD is "my refuge and my fortress" (Psalm 91:2), "my deliverer, / my God, my rock, in whom I take refuge, / my shield, and the horn of my salvation, my stronghold" (Psalm 18:2). What a metaphor: solid, high, impregnable, old, and enduring. You can't just hustle up to the top. There are perils up there. And yet spectacular views, rarefied air, proximity to...God? Heaven? How fit was Moses as an old man to scramble to such heights?

When the Israelites followed Moses (admittedly with much whining and grumbling!) into the desert and mountains of Sinai, they should have been grateful to have a guide who'd been there before, during his season of shepherding with father-in-law Jethro (Exodus 2:16-22). I've visited the world's oldest functioning monastery, St. Catherine's, which marks the spot where the relatively young Moses was spoken to by God from the burning bush. Interestingly enough, there is a massive bush within the monastery, encircled by sacred stones—still (as I remarked to my wife when we saw it) not consumed! That monastery was the home of Codex Sinaiticus, one of the oldest manuscripts of the Bible, and to several wonders of early Christian art, including the famous Christ Pantocrator. Rough craggy mountains loom over the place. Getting there by modern vehicle on recently paved roads takes hours. Moses the mountain man led the huge crowd there on foot.

And also beyond. The terrain just north of Mount Sinai, heading toward the Jordan River, is ragged, daunting, with plenty of crevices, clefts, caves, and places you could hide from the sun or your worst enemies. God sheltered Moses in such a cleft in the rock. And Christians who prayed this psalm meditated on clefts in mountains they'd visited and imagined them as the wounds in Jesus's crucified body. "Rock of ages, cleft for me, let me hide myself in thee."

We Have Laws

When God said goodbye and sent him back down the mountain, Moses bore the greatest souvenir, the grandest spiritual relic ever—so beautifully retold by Zora Neale Hurston:

> Moses lifted the freshly chiseled tablets of stone in his hands and gazed down the mountain to where Israel waited. He knew a great exultation. Now men could be free. They had something of the essence of divinity expressed. They had the chart and compass of behavior. They need not stumble into blind ways and injure themselves. This was bigger than Israel. It comprehended the world. Israel could be a heaven for all men forever, by these sacred stones. With flakes of light still clinging to his face, Moses turned to where Joshua waited for him. "Joshua, I have laws. Israel is going to know peace and justice."[5]

Those laws weren't the rulebook of a controlling deity, but an invitation, a road map for how freed people might stay free and thrive. They broke away from God's ways, as we do. The psalmist trembles in the shattering awareness that we have broken God's heart, and that we bear painful consequences for living sideways from God. Those consequences feel like God's wrath—which is what God's mercy feels like to us when it crashes into a wall we've erected instead of being welcomed through an open door. "By thy wrath we are overwhelmed" (Psalm 90:7).

Verse 8 shrewdly frets over "secret sins." We sin and keep it a secret—from others, and even from ourselves. Sin isn't just what we know we did wrongly. Often, it's sinning unawares. We hurt others without realizing it. We think some action is noble or holy, but it's out of sync with God. We have blind spots. Very pious slave owners used to pray, asking God how severely to punish a slave or whether to purchase more. The Lord has mercy even for our secret sins. The Lord would have them exposed and treated.

Notice verse 14's plea: "Oh, satisfy us early with Your mercy" (NKJV). Not just "Be merciful so I'm no longer in trouble." This very mercy satisfies. It is what satisfies us—not only with God but also in all relationships. Infants, the elderly, and the hurting: all of us crave, above all else, the mercy that satisfies.

Verse 13 asks for God to turn toward mercy. When the Israelites fashioned that golden calf, God's anger (understandably) raged against the people God had just delivered from bondage. But Moses pleaded to stave off the wrath, and God mercifully let God's people go—again. Mercy feels like God changing God's mind about us, God repenting.

While reflecting upon sin, Psalm 90 knits it tightly together with mortality. We segregate the two, and with some wisdom. Someone dies tragically, and we can be sure it was not because she did something to offend God that caused her demise. And yet one of our agonies in a sinful world is that some fair percentage of deaths is in fact due to sin, not just mine but also that of humanity. And I shudder when I ponder the connections between sin and spiritual death, that numbing feeling of being alive but not really dead to joy and hope.

Mortality

The high point (literally!) of Moses's story was the forty days spent alone with God on Mount Sinai. But a second climax (maybe something of an anticlimax) came years later on Mount Nebo, that summit perched high above the Jordan valley. I've taken busloads of pilgrims up its winding road to the top; the views are spectacular. How moved was Moses on arriving at that summit, where he could survey that vast, good, and promising land, his life's dream and that of his people spread out before him? It must have been a very clear day.

And then, his fabled life came to an abrupt, unwelcome halt. The moral here, the theological insight for all of us, was eloquently articulated by Reinhold Niebuhr: "Nothing that is worth doing can be achieved in our lifetime; therefore we must be saved by hope."[6] Our great privilege is to be part of something far larger than ourselves and extending beyond the short scope of even a long life. This is hope, this is our life with God, finding ourselves as a small but glorious piece of God's larger puzzle coming together.

Did Moses feel this kind of hope and satisfaction? If I were Moses, my heart would break irreparably. Did he die of literal heart failure? Mortality lurks behind every verse of Psalm 90—as it's always over your shoulder as you go about your business. For this psalmist, time is in God's hands, and so the end of each life also rests in God's hands— which is not to suggest that God zooms down and snatches your loved one from you, or even that the death of a loved one doesn't break your heart, or that your own impending death isn't devastating. When we get to Psalm 116, we'll say more about God and the hour of death. For now, we simply observe the profound honesty of Psalm 9 and the way that honesty has provided comfort through the ages.

Dietrich Bonhoeffer preached a tender, loving sermon on Psalm 90 at the funeral of his grandmother, pondering the passage of time and her and our need for refuge. "God has been very good to us in allowing her to be with us until now," and he was especially joyful she'd made it through Christmas! The hidden meaning of such a death for her surviving loved ones? "She transmitted to us the heritage of another age. With her passing a world passes, which we all in some way carry within us and want to keep within us."[7]

We not only *read* Psalm 90 at funerals. We often *sing* it. Isaac Watts fashioned its lines into one of his best hymns, "O God our Help in Ages Past"—who is "our hope for years to come, our shelter from the stormy blast, and our eternal home." Yes, inevitably, "Time, like an ever-flowing stream bears all its sons away."[8] *All.* Modern hymnals, trying to avoid the gender limitation of "sons" lunged for "bears all who breathe away," prompting an inside joke among members of my family. As it's sung, we catch one another's eyes, snicker, and think "but they're not breathing anymore."

We should all thank God that we have Scriptures and a church that isn't freaked out by death. We do not grieve as those who have no hope. The flood is mighty but cannot finally overwhelm us or God's good purposes. So the psalmist injects here and there little moments of hope in the thick of the weariness, despair, and lament.

Morning Has Broken

After swaying from confident expectation to hints of despair and then back to optimistic wisdom and yet again to shivers of despair, Psalm 90 finally settles on a finishing tone of hope and even joy—which may be the route we all must take to get to hope and joy! "Oh, satisfy us early with Your mercy, That we may rejoice and be glad all our days!" (v. 14, NKJV). Christian ears perk up when we hear "early," as we hang our yearnings and identity on that morning when the tomb turned up empty.

But in a way, even in Old Testament times (which knew nothing of resurrection or eternal life), morning had its theological richness. In the wilderness, Moses's people peeked out every morning to find newly fallen manna to sustain them. Many Jews to this day, on waking, say "Thanks" as their first word. The rising sun was literally not just a new day but also symbolized a new beginning. Morning is like that: a little Easter, a fresh start, and a new creation.

Is there any subtle clue in these words, even falling on Israelite ears, that there might be more after time bears us all away? Does verse 15 tease out a glimmer of hope beyond, looking for days to balance or outnumber days of affliction and evil? We mentioned that the mood of Psalm 90 sometimes reminds us of Ecclesiastes, where all the work you do, no matter how impressive or substantial, eventually comes to nothing. Our psalm prays, in fresh hope, "Establish thou the work of our hands" (v. 17). Make it matter. Make it endure. What was the period, the exclamation mark Paul put on his great chapter on resurrection? "Be steadfast, immovable, always abounding in the work of the Lord, knowing that in the Lord your labor is not in vain" (1 Corinthians 15:58).

Indeed, the psalm's closing verse states, "Let the favor of the Lord our God be upon us." That word *favor* could as easily be rendered "beauty." How to wind up a psalm or a life? "Let the beauty of the Lord our God be upon us." The writers of the Old Testament knew well and were moved by the beauty of the Lord. But then we Christians know the fullness of the beauty of the Lord. "Fairest Lord Jesus, Beautiful Savior." And the beauty of the Body of Christ, the beauty of the lives of Christ's saints, and the simple joy and exquisite delight in our life with God, now and in eternity, the prayer of Psalm 90:14 elegantly answered "that we may rejoice and be glad all our days."

What is the "message" (if you will) of Psalm 90 in a nutshell? I admire my friend Wesley Vander Lugt's sermon on this text, the heart of which was this threefold assurance: "God is home no matter how restless we feel; God is creator no matter how chaotic the world seems; God is eternal no matter how fleeting our life may be."[9]

Living with Moses

A footnote: when I think of Moses, the image I visualize is not Charlton Heston, great as he was in Cecil B. DeMille's *The Ten Commandments*, but rather Michelangelo's stunning sculpture, which resides to the right of the high altar in a church up on the Esquiline Hill in Rome, the Basilica of St. Peter in Chains. I've been close enough to touch it—and this Moses is big, really big, nearly eight feet tall while seated. In the three dimensionality of the room, that mass of solid stone pulsates with energy, as if Moses is about to turn or stand. Simply magnificent, titanic, of commanding authority, his gaze piercing. The commandments he's holding? His look makes me sure to keep them.

Of course, Michelangelo's Moses has horns. In this impressive statue, the horns look, if anything, imposing, like antennae or powerful appendages. This notion of Moses with horns was the result of Latin translators mistranslating the Hebrew of Exodus 34:29: they mistook "the skin of his face shone" and rendered it "his face had horns," the two options differing by only a slight flick of the pen. Later, as anti-Semitism took hold among deluded Christians, Moses and many Jews were depicted as having horns, like demons. I like to think Michelangelo was not fond of this idea, but he kept the horns.

Pope Julius had hired him to carve this sculpture for his tomb, but other projects kept distracting Michelangelo so that it took more than three decades to complete the project. His workshop was his home— and so, as art historian William Wallace puts it, "Michelangelo lived with Moses; the two grew old together. Every morning the artist woke up with Moses. Every time he returned home, he was welcomed by the same imposing figure. To live with Moses could be unnerving."[10]

Psalm 90, written by Moses or perceived as so fitting him that later editors attached his name to it, invites us to live with and grow old with Moses and the themes that constituted his life. Wallace made me chuckle when describing the day they finally transported that massive statue three miles, from Michelangelo's home to the St. Peter in Chains church: "A few astonished persons stood gaping as Moses, peering over the side of a rude cart, slowly rolled through the streets of Rome."[11]

6
Psalm 116

Love: Precious in the Sight of the Lord

6

Psalm 116

Love: Precious in the Sight of the Lord

We know, from Matthew 26:30 and from everything else we know about Jewish Passover meals, that Jesus and the disciples sang in the upper room at the Last Supper. I try to imagine what they sounded like. What was the tune, the melody? Did they harmonize? Was Jesus a bass, baritone, or tenor? Was his voice strong with vibrato or more plaintive? Did he lead? Or was Nathaniel or maybe one of the sons of Zebedee the reliable one to start on key? No instruments we know of, so it was a cappella, and I'd guess in a room of stone flooring and walls, so with long reverb time. Jesus and his disciples, vocalizing, then hearing their own voices resonating for a few seconds after they'd stopped. I'm moved when I ponder this.

We can't be sure how they sounded, but we know what they sang—and it wasn't the bawdy, slightly drunken "Always thought that I'd be an apostle, knew that I could make it if I tried" from *Jesus Christ Superstar*. They sang psalms. And we know which ones. Psalms 113–118 were prescribed for Passover. Six great psalms! But consider the context: Jesus and his closest friends on their last night together, singing these six?

How emotional and haunting was it for Jesus, and maybe even the still-clueless disciples, to sing aloud so many poignant lines on such a night? "Out of my distress I called on the Lord.... What can man do to me?" (Psalm 118:5-6). "All nations surrounded me" (v. 10). "I shall not die, but I shall live" (v. 17). "The Lord has chastened me sorely, / but he has not given me over to death" (v. 18). "The stone which the builders rejected / has become the head of the corner" (v. 22). "This is the day which the Lord has made" (v. 24)—which in their language would have meant something like "This is the day on which the Lord has acted." The disciples were thinking of Passover and deliverance from Egypt. Was Jesus weighing the chances that the Lord's act on this day would be his sacrificial death?

The most heartrending among those psalms they sang had to be Psalm 116. "The snares of death encompassed me" (v. 3). "O Lord, I beseech thee, save my life!" (v. 4). Did Jesus repeat these words a couple of hours later in Gethsemane? "For thou hast delivered my soul from death, / my eyes from tears, / my feet from stumbling" (v. 8). "I will lift up the cup of salvation" (v. 13)—which he'd just done with the Passover wine. "Precious in the sight of the Lord / is the death of his saints" (v. 15). They knew these words by heart, but was Jesus the only one who sensed death was lurking outside?

The Upper Room

Where did they sing these psalms together? We cannot be sure. Pilgrims have for centuries now been directed to an upstairs room just outside the old city walls of Jerusalem on Mount Zion. Called the Cenacle, it is plenty picturesque, even if its architecture and decorations give it away as being centuries newer than wherever Jesus and the disciples ate.

Pastor and professor Fred Craddock used to tell a great story about touring the site. While his group waited their turn to enter, a pastor with a deep, earnest spirituality was telling his group, "This is the very room where Jesus shared the Last Supper. You're sitting on the very seats the disciples sat on. This is the very table..." All very moving. They had a prayer and exited. Then Craddock's guide brought his group in and explained, "You can tell from the arched ceiling and the masonry walls that this room is fourteenth century or later." A woman next to Craddock whispered to him, "I wish I were in the other group."

The Cenacle can frustrate anyone expecting a spiritual high. Loud groups shove their way over you, people taking selfies, the touristy feel crushing whatever you came wishing for. But once, I got my group alone in there for a few minutes. We made a large circle around the edges—and just as I was about to utter something I was sure would be profound, a large group in colored African finery flooded into the open space we'd created, bowed their heads, and began to sing in a powerful, luscious harmony, allowing rests for their intonations to reverberate, then singing even more deeply. They were embracing one another, many in tears, and some of them began embracing us. Surely the presence of the Lord was in this place. One bread, one body. Jesus's gift of immense beauty across space and time.

Let's step back in time from the Cenacle today, and wherever Jesus and his closest ones sang, back into Old Testament times. Originally, Psalm 116 was a song of thanksgiving. Someone who had been in dire straits came into the temple to make a thank offering and did so in the presence of other friends, family, and even strangers who'd come for worship. The psalm was so eloquent that its words stuck, were recorded on scrolls, repeated, and memorized by generations. One fortunate person's prayer provides the words for countless others—to strengthen their hope in seasons of despair and to demonstrate how to give thanks and keep whatever promises you made to God when you were in a mess if God would only get you out of the mess. Derek Kidner rightly says, "There is an infectious delight and touching gratitude about this psalm."[1]

As we read, a glimmer of a "maybe" might pop into your head: maybe this psalm will solve that nagging problem of evil, of that nagging question of why bad things happen. As we'll see, the psalm does even better, truer work for us. Jason Byassee is spot on: "There is no 'answer' to the 'problem of evil.' But prayers this gritty can make for a hardy people, unsurprised at suffering or at seeing God's goodness from the depths."[2]

And singing isn't just something we enjoy. Singing God's songs really matters, especially in times of mortal danger and moral peril. Bull Connor, that racist commissioner of public safety in Birmingham during the Civil Rights Movement, was enraged by the Freedom Riders, manhandling them off the Trailways bus, egging on the mob that was brutalizing the riders with bats and iron pipes, and then throwing them all in jail, swearing they'd never get out. But the next day, he relented and put them back on the bus headed out of town. Asked why he changed his mind, he said, "I just couldn't stand their singing."[3] Evil cowers before the hardy people of God singing words of hope and joy.

I Love the Lord

So let us take a stroll through Psalm 116, just a word or phrase at a time, reading slowly—as God intends. Verse 1 is itself so profound, so spiritually inviting, that we could fill the rest of this book exploring its many facets. "I love the LORD, because he has heard / my voice." When God made me, you, and the rest of us, what did God yearn to get in return? God being God doesn't need anything from us, but God being a personal God longs for a response, a reply to God's being and goodness. We may have heard God wants fear or reverence, or God wants us to behave or to fund God's projects down here, or God is just waiting for us to ask for favors God can grant, or God wants obedience or sacrifice or even faith. All these have some small purchase on what God is looking for.

But at the heart of it all, the God who is love above all else craves just that from us: love. God loves. And if we have any even dim glimpse of how deep and enduring that love is, we cannot help but love God in reply. And yet, we might just not love. In its many manifestations, sin is nothing but a simple failure to love God. God is supremely lovable. Many of our hymns resound with expressions of love.

Israel's primal command, recited constantly by memory, is "Hear, O Israel:... you shall love the LORD your God..." (Deuteronomy 6:4-5).

Did you catch the connection between hearing and love? Our psalmist loves—for many reasons! Let me count the ways! But first in line? "I love the LORD, because he has heard my voice." Hear O Israel. Listen to the God who listens. "I love the Lord because he listened," not because God did what I wanted! God simply heard. Isn't that our deepest craving? To be heard? Understood? Noticed? Cared for? Love is listening. Listening is love. More on this later.

For God so loved the world that God gave God's Son. Jesus, lover of my soul, loved his disciples, the poor, total strangers, and even those who despised him. He forgave the very soldiers who'd thrust nails through his pure, holy body and were gambling over his garments at the foot of the cross. They'd not even asked or understood; Jesus loved even them. Jesus kissed Judas in the thick of his betrayal and called him "friend."

I am deeply moved when I realize Peter was in that room when Jesus muttered sadly that his dearest would betray him. Peter swore he'd never do such a thing! But then he did, not once but three times. Yet then, the resurrected Jesus, after cooking breakfast for the disciples, asked Peter not once but three times—not "Are you sorry?" or "Didn't I tell you?" or "How could you?" but simply, "Do you love me?" (John 21:15-17). That's what Jesus wants to know from me, from you—and "yes" is enough. Thomas Merton's simple prayer always keeps me focused: "Let this be my only consolation, that wherever I am You, my Lord, are loved."[4]

James Mays reads Psalm 116 as a "declaration of love."[5] Indeed, the psalm as a whole, as he reads it so wisely, illustrates what form love assumes, a summary of how we love, why we love, and how we might love more purely. It's fivefold! Love calls the beloved by name (v. 4). Love finds rest in the beloved (v. 7). Love lives always as if in the presence of the beloved (v. 9). Love serves the beloved (v. 16). And love fulfills its vows to the beloved (v. 14), those promises made in public—and kept. That last thought reminds me of Lewis Smedes's great observation:

> Yes, somewhere people still make and keep promises. They choose not to quit when the going gets rough.... They stick to lost causes. They hold on to a love grown cold. They stay with people who have become pains in the neck. They still dare to make promises and care enough to keep the promises they make. I want to say to you that if you have a ship you will not desert, if you have people you will not forsake, if you have causes you will not abandon, then *you are like God.* [6]

Here's a quirky Hebrew thing. The original text of verse 1 doesn't actually say "I love the Lord." It simply says, "I love." The context makes it clear—but intriguing, isn't it, to consider the possibility that I love... not just God but all the possible objects of my love, because the Lord has listened to me. Being heard, being known, being cared for: doesn't this liberate us to love others or to love God's world? If the recipient of love here is left dangling, then we can get outside our self-interest and love, filling in the blanks any old way. I love (there it is!) Beth Nielsen Chapman's song "How We Love," which tells us, "All that matters in the end is how we love."[7]

Verse 2 teases us with a tender image of God's hearing. God has "inclined his ear to me." Some overly literal intellectuals might object that God, being God, has no ears. But ask the one who's prayed, who's suffered, and who's trusted in and been aided by God. Spurgeon envisions God "as a tender physician or loving friend leaning over a sick man whose voice is faint and scarcely audible, so as to catch every accent and whisper." Indeed, "When our prayer is very feeble, so that we ourselves scarcely hear it, and question whether we do pray or not, yet God bows a listening ear."[8] Since God is such a tender healer, bending over to listen to even a feeble whisper or a sigh, "I will call on him as long as I live" (v. 2). And why not? On his deathbed, John Wesley retrieved from his fading memory an Isaac Watts hymn and sang "I'll Praise My Maker While I've Breath."[9]

Near-Death Experience

What was it the bent, tender Lord heard with that divine ear? "The snares of death encompassed me; / the pangs of Sheol laid hold on me" (v. 3). Have you ever been near death? Was there a time you thought you might not make it, but you did? I thought I was in fine health until one evening at a fundraising reception my stomach hurt a little, and then a lot, and finally I was doubled over in tears and moans, prompting my wife to drive me to the emergency room.

After only a few minutes, a surgeon was in front of me, saying, "Sir, you need surgery."

Shocked, as I'd expected a pill or an IV, I asked, "When?"

She said, "Right now."

Dizzied by this, I inquired, "Can't we wait until tomorrow morning?"

She grimly said, "Sir, you could die tonight."

I wish I could say that, after a grueling two weeks in the hospital and a long recovery, I'm a different person now, more grateful, more tender, making the most of my days. I approximate that now and then; I've tried not to return to normal. Henri Nouwen wrote a little book abounding in wisdom about the time he was struck by a car and nearly died. *Our Greatest Gift* is about how to befriend death before it arrives; how as the children of God, death's power over us has been stripped away; how as we age God might be glorified in our weakness; how to focus on a life that is less about productivity and more about being fruitful, attentive to what will survive and even thrive after we are gone.

My question, Have you ever been near death? is a little bit absurd. You, I, and everybody else are near death all day, every day. If you go out of the house, especially if you get into an automobile, you are perilously near death every minute, hurled as you are through traffic, trusting total strangers who are stressed or texting or of that other political party (so you suspect they are a bit deranged). Who knows what time bomb is ticking inside your body?

And then there's the death that settles upon and within us even while your heart is still beating and you're out and about. The walking dead. Vapid lives, going through the motions, numb to reality, coping. Scripture names this kind of death that riddles us this side of the grave. "You were dead" (Ephesians 2:1; see also Colossians 2:13). Not dead yet, but dead enough.

Father Murphy tantalized his students when lecturing on the way death in the Bible isn't just when your heart stops beating. Rather, it is a dynamic power, pursuing you all your days, reaching up (and he would extend his very long, wiry arm to illustrate) from the depths of Sheol, threatening to drag you down. His friend and Psalms scholar James Mays wrote of death as "a sphere of power that invades the realm of the living and entangles life."[10]

Our psalmist: he sounds as if he teetered on the precipice of physical death, but who knows? Maybe his spirit was entirely deflated. Maybe his relationships were broken, like a field of dead bones. The people of Israel more than once were at the point of death. Hopeless. No way forward. Maybe it's only when there's no hope that we hope against hope and open up to the only real hope. "Then I called on the name of the LORD: / 'O LORD, I beseech thee, save my life!' / ... when I was brought low, he saved me. / ... For thou hast delivered my soul from death" (vv. 4, 6, 8).

The Lord Saved Me

Notice the words *then* and *saved* in the verse above. *Then* the psalmist called on the Lord? I'm guessing this psalmist did so regularly. But for many, only the *then* spurs us to call on the Lord, like a 911 call, when we are in big trouble. The Lord does not mind. But the Lord wants to hear from us often, daily, constantly, like a real relationship of love. And God hopes we'll buy into what Isaac Bashevis Singer cleverly noticed: "Whenever I am in trouble, I pray. And since I'm always in trouble, I pray a lot."[11]

The psalmist was "saved." For many churchgoers, that sounds as if he accepted Christ and secured his entry into heaven, whether he died now or not. Our psalmist wasn't thinking, *Believe, accept, so if and when you die you'll go to heaven.* He means he *was* saved. God used my surgeon to save my life. God tapped that driver on the shoulder so he didn't drift over the line and collide with me head-on. God reached down and staved off a heart attack or used a dear friend to love me enough to persuade me not to take my own life. However, we conceive of things, we're eyeing here a humbled one who was very close to death, physical or spiritual, but was saved and now lives on.

If you're reading this, you've lived on. How do we live on? With a deep awareness of being saved, having made it when we might not have. And with, of course, a constant (as best you can manage!) gratitude. Maybe gentler. Wiser. And more prayerful. Less praying for things and more simply praying—time with God, resting in God's presence. Praising. Precious time with God. So many psalms plead with God and even motivate God to save their lives precisely so they can praise God, because for them, if you'll recall, when you die, you're dead. No more talking with God! So as long as you're alive, you talk with God while you still can.

And then, of course, being one who was saved, whose desperate prayers played some part in the fortunate outcome, you then pray for others and for the world. The Hebrew in verse 4 of our psalm is emphatic, meaning, "I prayed, and kept on praying." We Americans tend to expect quick replies to our quick prayers. But the saints of old have much to teach us about the value of the long labor of prayer. Monica prayed for so long, with the intensity of tears for her beloved son (who later became Augustine). Ambrose, spying on Monica over a very long time, declared that "it's impossible that the son of these tears of yours will perish."[12] And I love George Buttrick's vivid image of prayer as beating on heaven's door "with bruised knuckles in the dark."[13] Prayer isn't efficient. And God isn't checking his watch, waiting for you to log enough time before answering. It's a relationship, and every relationship requires and is blessed by the faithful, enduring investment of time, energy, and love.

'Tis a Gift to be Simple

I love verse 6: "The LORD preserves the simple." This is similar to how Jesus put it in his Beatitudes: "Blessed are the meek" (Matthew 5:5). In Psalm 116:6, the Hebrew word translated "simple" (*pata'im*) implies the naive, the gullible, the vulnerable, and the helpless. Such hope! God isn't a big booster of the high-control power people but of the weak. In fact, the Greek translation of the Hebrew Bible, known as the Septuagint, says that the Lord preserves *nepia*—babes! God preserves the most vulnerable of all, mere infants—which is the gospel!—as God became for us so very small, as a mere infant, as simple as every single person once was in infancy.

So much American thinking is about taking care of ourselves. In Flannery O'Connor's marvelous short story "A Good Man Is Hard to Find," a violent man holds up a family during their travels. Terrified but full of faith, the older woman tells him that if he would just pray, Jesus would help him. "I don't want no hep," he says. "I'm doing all right by myself."[14]

But he is not, just as we all can get frantic, anxious, and weary trying to go it alone. Realizing his total dependence upon God for his very life, the psalmist talks to himself: "Return, O my soul, to your rest" (Psalm 116:7). Moses understood God's long strategy to bring Israel to a place of rest. Creation's entire purpose was that sabbath day of rest. It's not laziness or doing nothing for God. It's the calm, the balance—as if the psalmist could overhear Jesus in the distant future inviting us: "Come to me, all who labor and are heavy laden, and I will give you rest" (Matthew 11:28).

Our psalmist kept his faith (v. 10), perhaps after almost losing it (as in Psalm 73), and survived—to his surprise! "I walk before the LORD / in the land of the living" (v. 9). Not "I go back to my old way of life"! Now "I walk before the Lord," cognizant I almost didn't make it, attuned to the presence of the Lord, the only reality that really matters at the end of the day. Not that the psalmist believes for one second that God will always rescue him or that he will never suffer any harm. God quite clearly doesn't insulate us from danger; God isn't a bubble to keep trouble at bay.

How Much Do I Owe You?

Dumbstruck and pulsating with gratitude, the psalmist asks the one question we'd all be wise to ask to figure out our mission for the rest of our lives—or just for today: "What shall I render to the LORD for all his bounty to me?" (v. 12). Of course, no offering, no sacrifice, and no mountain of doing for God would be sufficient. And yet we now know we are here to render all we have, even our very selves to the Lord. I love Don Schlitz's great song, popularized by Tanya Tucker, Paul Davis, and Paul Overstreet. A husband asks his wife what he owes her for standing beside him: Diamonds? Furs? Then a son asks his mother the same question. Their answer is the same as the one the Lord gives when the man asks God how much he owes for God granting him his life and all that is in it. And the Lord said, "I won't take less than your love, sweet love. No, I won't take less than your love."[15]

Our psalmist answers his own question, "What shall I render to the LORD?" with a simple, profound gesture: "I will lift up the cup of salvation" (vv. 12-13). Remember we are in the courts of the Jewish temple, watching the rescued one telling friends, family, and onlookers his story. And then he literally raises a cup, brimming with wine. Does he drink and share? Does he pour it out on the ground as a worshipful emptying of himself in thanks to God? We read of such drink offerings in Numbers 28:7; Genesis 25:14; and Leviticus 23:13.

I admire Kidner's comment on verses 12 and 13: "The New Testament itself could hardly give a better glimpse than this of heaven's grace and man's response."[16] But we do get a vivid glimpse when our hearts and minds relocate themselves into that upper room and Jesus's last night, his last meal with his disciples—when they sang these very words together. Jesus lifted up the cup of salvation and told them, "This is my blood" (Matthew 26:28). He'd just broken the bread. I'm sure as he tore the bread, he caught a glimpse of what would happen to his body, and soon. So with the cup as well. As Jesus stared into that wine, he caught a vision of his own blood, which would be shed, and soon.

But his shed blood, that greatest of all unjust tragedies, wasn't tragic forever. God redeemed him, and us. His blood, shed not ingloriously but gloriously for us, all of us, the salvation of the world. That is what Jesus rendered to God his Father and to us, his brothers and sisters. We know he raised that cup as he sang the very words of our psalm. Did his mind also meander back to our beloved Twenty-Third Psalm? "My cup overflows" (v. 5). Overflowing—with sorrow? Or love mingled down? Or zeal for God? Or pangs for his mother?

Those who ate, drank, and sang with Jesus in that upper room were baffled, with only the first dim hints of what was to come and what it would mean. As Austin Farrer put it: "Jesus gave his body and blood to his disciples in bread and wine. Amazed at such a token, and little understanding what they did, Peter, John and the rest reached out their hands and took their master and their God. Whatever else they knew or did not know, they knew they were committed to him ... and that they, somehow, should live it out."[17]

Precious in the Sight of the Lord

Finally, in verse 15, we come to the psalm's (and all of Scripture's) climax: "Precious in the sight of the LORD / is the death of his saints." Let's be clear: our psalmist, like all other authors of the Bible, does not say God causes death. In our agony, we ask, Why did God take my husband? But God does not take life. God grieves the loss of life. After his son died when his car plummeted into Boston Harbor, William Sloane Coffin preached a sermon in which he declared,

The night after Alex died, I was sitting in the living room of my sister's house outside of Boston, when the front door opened and in came a nice-looking middle-aged woman, carrying about eighteen quiches. When she saw me she shook her head, then headed for the kitchen, saying sadly over her shoulder, "I just don't understand the will of God." Instantly I was up and in hot pursuit, swarming all over her. "I'll say you don't, lady!" I said. (I knew the anger would do me good, and the instruction to her was long overdue.) I continued, "Do you think it was the will of God that Alex never fixed that lousy windshield wiper on his car? ... That there are no streetlights along that stretch of road, and no guardrail separating the road and Boston Harbor?"

For some reason, nothing so infuriates me as the incapacity of seemingly intelligent people to get it through their heads that God doesn't go around this world with his finger on triggers, his fist around knives, his hands on steering wheels. . . . The one thing that should never be said when someone dies is, "It is the will of God." Never do we know enough to say that. My own consolation lies in knowing that it was not the will of God that Alex die; that when the waves closed over the sinking car, God's heart was the first of all our hearts to break.[18]

Death is precious in the eyes of the Lord. The Lord saw and sees and bears. The Hebrew word translated "precious" also carries the connotation of "costly." When someone you love and can't imagine living without dies, your heart is broken, shattered. We take some consolation in such a moment that God is in solidarity with us, the divine heart aching with sorrow. Indeed, Jason Byassee speaks truly: "The death of a faithful person is precious (not just painful) because it imitates and participates in Christ's victory over death"[19]—his costly death, the one Jesus died after eating and drinking and singing our psalm with his disciples. If we include martyrs, those put to death for standing up for God, such a grievous death is exceedingly precious to God.

Even on the human plane, the death of those we love can be precious. On the surface, death seems to be the antithesis of "precious." But I know so many people who have been by the bedside of a loved one at the moment of death—and there is a beauty, a tenderness, a wonder. Surely for God, who envelops the dying in a welcoming embrace, death is precious. And by "saints," the Hebrew word *hasīd* doesn't mean an officially sanctioned saint like Francis or a dogged, holy hero like Dorothy Day. The *hasīd*, whose death is precious in the eyes of the Lord is the loyal, devoted follower, the one who prays, seeks

God, tries their best, believes, and in extremity knows of nothing else to do but to place life themself into God's strong, loving hands.

Deathbed scenes, stories, and memories intrigue me. What did he say at the end? What did our final embrace feel like? We long—for ourselves, and for those we love—for a good death: peaceful, not alone, surrounded by loved ones, maybe even singing a hymn. John Wesley, after lingering in silence for a long time, surprised those watching over his deathbed by singing Isaac Watts's hymn "I'll Praise my Maker While I Have Breath." The great theologian Thomas Aquinas heard a voice from above: "Thomas, you have spoken well of me. What reward would you ask for?" He replied, "Nothing but yourself, O Lord." Of course, so many deaths are sudden, unwelcomed, and horrifying. God alone is able to redeem and shed the divine dignity on them all when we can only shiver and weep.

Our psalmist, saved and on intimate terms with God, fears death no longer. He has befriended death—which is coming for all of us. The beauty of the church is that we are not frightened by death, the dead, the dying, or those grieving. We catch glimpses of the hope and the beauty. In the church, like nowhere else, death has this precious quality. We know how God values and treasures our saints who are gone and how the saving goes on. Fractured relationships are reforged and turned joyful. The broken are made whole. The depressed and forlorn dance for joy. And ultimately, death, being so precious to God, is that moment when God not only draws us close into God's own presence; as we step into eternity, God makes us like God. "Beloved, we are God's children now; it does not yet appear what we shall be, but we know that when he appears we shall be like him" (1 John 3:2).

Notes

Introduction

1   Thomas Merton, *Praying the Psalms* (Collegeville: Liturgical Press, 1956), 7–8.
2   Dietrich Bonhoeffer, *Psalms: The Prayerbook of the Bible*, trans. James H. Burtness (Minneapolis: Augsburg, 1970), 9–11.
3   Niall Williams, *History of the Rain* (New York: Bloomsbury, 2014), 337.
4   Walter Brueggemann, *Abiding Astonishment: Psalms, Modernity, and the Making of History* (Louisville: Westminster John Knox, 1991), 26.

Chapter 1

1   Dacher Keltner, *Awe: The New Science of Everyday Wonder and How It Can Transform Your Life* (New York: Penguin, 2023), 18.
2   Keltner, *Awe*, 128.
3   Charles Spurgeon, *The Treasury of David* (Peabody, MA: Hendrickson, n.d.), vol. 1, 79.
4   Thomas Merton, *New Seeds of Contemplation* (New York: New Directions, 1961), 29.
5   Henri J. M. Nouwen, *The Inner Voice of Love: A Journey Through Anguish to Freedom* (New York: Doubleday, 1998), 3.
6   Nouwen, *Inner Voice of Love*, 4.
7   Daniel O. Snyder, *Praying in the Dark: Spirituality, Nonviolence, and the Emerging World* (Eugene, OR: Cascade, 2022), 9, 13.
8   Niall Williams, *This Is Happiness* (New York: Bloomsbury, 2019), 33.
9   Samantha Harvey, *Orbital* (New York: Grove, 2023), 63.
10 Harvey, *Orbital*, 107.
11 Mother Teresa, *My Life for the Poor* (San Francisco: Harper & Row, 1985), 20.
12 Peter Craigie, *Psalms 1–50* (Grand Rapids, MI: Zondervan, 1984), 108.
13 Barbara Brown Taylor, *Bread of Angels* (New York: Cowley, 1997), 31–35.
14 Madeleine L'Engle, *A Cry Like a Bell* (Wheaton, IL: Harold Shaw, 2000), 55.

Chapter 2

1   Wesley Vander Lugt, *Beauty Is Oxygen: Finding a Faith That Breathes* (Grand Rapids, MI: Eerdmans, 2024), 16.

2   Fyodor Dostoevsky, *The Idiot*, trans. Alan Myers (New York: Oxford University Press, 1992), 402.

3   Joseph August Seiss (lyrics trans., 1873), "Fairest Lord Jesus," *The United Methodist Hymnal* (Nashville: Abingdon, 1989), #189.

4   Augustine, *Expositions of the Psalms*, vol. 2, trans. Maria Boulding (El Segundo, CA: New City, 2000), 283.

5   Niall Williams, *Time of the Child* (New York: Bloomsbury, 2024), 248.

6   Wesley Vander Lugt, ed., *A Prophet in the Darkness: Exploring Theology in the Art of Georges Rouault* (Downers Grove, IL: Intervarsity, 2024), xii.

7   Marilynne Robinson, *Gilead* (New York: Farrar, Straus and Giroux, 2004), 137.

8   Ellen Charry, *Psalms 1–50* (Grand Rapids, MI: Brazos, 2015), 138.

9   Twila Paris (lyrics), "How Beautiful," track 6 on Twila Paris, *Cry for the Desert*, Star Song Records, 1990.

10 Frederick Buechner, *The Clown in the Belfry: Writings on Faith and Fiction* (San Francisco: Harper, 1992), 158.

11 Lorraine Hansberry, *A Raisin in the Sun* (New York: Random House, 1959), 36.

12 Ken Follett, *The Pillars of the Earth* (New York: Penguin, 1989), 18.

13 Vander Lugt, *Beauty Is Oxygen*, 49.

14 Robert Alter, *The Book of Psalms* (New York: W. W. Norton, 2007), 92.

Chapter 3

1   Bonhoeffer, *Psalms*, 14–15.

2   Chris E. W. Green, *Being Transfigured: Lenten Homilies* (Abbotsford, BC: St. Macrina, 2023), 97.

3   Thomas O. Chisholm (lyrics, 1923), "Great Is Thy Faithfulness," *The United Methodist Hymnal* (Nashville: Abingdon, 1989), #140.

4   James Allison, *Undergoing God: Dispatches from the Scene of a Break-In* (New York: Continuum, 2006), 113.

5   Christian Wiman, *Zero at the Bone: Fifty Entries Against Despair* (New York: Farrar, Straus and Giroux, 2023), 37.

6   Spurgeon, *The Treasury of David*, vol. 1, 401.

7   Spurgeon, *The Treasury of David*, vol. 1, 408.

8   Lauren Winner, *The Dangers of Christian Practice: On Wayward Gifts, Characteristic Damage, and Sin* (New Haven: Yale University Press, 2018), 82.

9   Dietrich Bonhoeffer, *Life Together*, trans. Daniel Bloesch and James Burtness (Philadelphia: Fortress, 1996), 110.

10 Spurgeon, *The Treasury of David*, vol. 1, 409.

11 Adelaide A. Potter (lyrics, 1902), "Have Thine Own Way Lord," *The United Methodist Hymnal* (Nashville: Abingdon, 1989), #382. This version changes the verse in question to, "Wash me just now, Lord, wash me just now." The original can be seen in, for example, *African Methodist Episcopal Church Hymnal* (Nashville: African Methodist Episcopal Church, 2011), #345.

Notes

12   C. S. Lewis, *Letters to Malcolm: Chiefly on Prayer* (New York: Harcourt Brace, 1963), 146.

13   "A Bidding Prayer," in *The Book of Occasional Services* (New York: Church Publishing, 2004), 32.

Chapter 4

1   Walter Brueggemann, *The Message of the Psalms* (Minneapolis, MN: Augsburg, 1984), 115.

2   Spurgeon, *The Treasury of David*, vol. 2, 247.

3   Derek Kidner, *Psalms 73–150* (Downers Grove, IL: IVP Academic, 2014), 290.

4   C. S. Lewis, *The Problem of Pain* (London: Macmillan, 1940), 81. In the film *Shadowlands*, Lewis (played by Anthony Hopkins) vividly pounded his fist into his other palm as he spoke of God's hammer blows.

5   Annie Dillard, *Teaching a Stone to Talk: Expeditions and Encounters* (New York: Harper Perennial, 1982), 58.

6   Jan Karon, *At Home in Mitford* (New York: Penguin, 1996), 203.

7   Dietrich Bonhoeffer, *Letters and Papers from Prison*, ed. Eberhard Bethge (New York: Macmillan, 1953), 157.

8   This was my church family's Advent prayer for 2020, created by Rev. Taylor Pryde Barefoot.

9   John Goldingay, *The First Testament: A New Translation* (Downers Grove, IL: IVP Academic, 2018), 564.

Chapter 5

1   Quoted from a conversation with Robert McAfee Brown in *Spirituality and Liberation: Overcoming the Great Fallacy* (Philadelphia: Westminster, 1988), 136.

2   Bryan Stevenson, *Just Mercy: A Story of Justice and Redemption* (New York: One World, 2014), 17.

3   Kidner, *Psalms 73–150*, 359.

4   Spurgeon, *The Treasury of David*, vol. 2, 61.

5   Zora Neale Hurston, *Moses, Man of the Mountain* (New York: Harper Perennial, 1991), 233.

6   Reinhold Niebuhr, *The Irony of American History* (New York: Charles Scribner's Sons, 1952), 63.

7   Dietrich Bonhoeffer, *Meditating on the Word*, ed. David McI. Gracie (New York: Ballantine, 1986), 68, 70.

8   Isaac Watts (lyric, 1719), "O God, Our Help in Ages Past," *The United Methodist Hymnal* (Nashville: Abingdon, 1989), 117.

9   Wesley Vander Lugt, unpublished sermon manuscript, August 2024.

10   William E. Wallace, *Michelangelo, God's Architect: The Story of His Final Years and Greatest Masterpiece* (Princeton: Princeton University Press, 2019), 9.

11   Wallace, *Michelangelo, God's Architect*, 9.

Chapter 6

1   Derek Kidner, *Psalms 73–150*, 442.

2   Jason Byassee, *Psalms 101–150* (Grand Rapids, MI: Brazos, 2018), 110.

3   David Greenberg, *John Lewis: A Life* (New York: Simon & Schuster, 2024), 79.

4   Thomas Merton, *Thoughts in Solitude* (New York: Noonday, 1956), 99.

5   James L. Mays, *Psalms* (Louisville, KY: John Knox, 1994), 371.

6   Lewis B. Smedes, "The Power of Promises," in *A Chorus of Witnesses: Model Sermons for Today's Preacher*, ed. Thomas G. Long and Cornelius Plantinga Jr. (Grand Rapids, MI: Eerdmans, 1994), 156 (emphasis original).

7   Beth Nielsen Chapman (lyrics), "How We Love," track 4 on Beth Nielsen Chapman, *Back to Love*, BNC Records, 2010.

8   Spurgeon, *The Treasury of David*, vol. 3, 67.

9   Stanley Ayling, *John Wesley* (Nashville: Abingdon, 1979), 315.

10   Mays, *Psalms*, 370–71.

11   Morton A. Reichek, "'Yiddish,' Says Isaac Bashevis Singer, 'Contains Vitamins that Other Languages Don't Have,'" *New York Times*, March 23, 1975, https://www.nytimes.com/1975/03/23/archives/yiddish-says-isaac-bashevis-singer-contains-vitamins-that-other.html.

12   Augustine, *Confessions*, trans. Sarah Ruden (New York: Modern Library, 2017), 74.

13   George Arthur Buttrick, *Prayer* (Nashville, Abingdon, 1977), 36.

14   Flannery O'Connor, "A Good Man Is Hard to Find," in *A Good Man Is Hard to Find and Other Stories* (San Diego, CA: Harvest, 1955), 26.

15   Paul Overstreet and Don Schlitz (lyrics), "I Won't Take Less Than Your Love," featuring Paul Overstreet and Paul Davis, track 3 on Tanya Tucker, *Love Me like You Used To*, Capitol, 1987.

16   Kidner, *Psalms 73–150*, 445.

17   Austin Farrer, *The Crown of the Year: Weekly Paragraphs for the Holy Sacrament* (Westminster, UK: Dacre, 1952), 9.

18   William Sloane Coffin, "Alex's Death," in *This Incomplete One: Words Occasioned by the Death of a Young Person*, ed. Michael D. Bush (Grand Rapids, MI: Eerdmans, 2006), 56–57.

19   Jason Byassee, *Psalms 101–150* (Grand Rapids, MI: Brazos, 2018), 108.

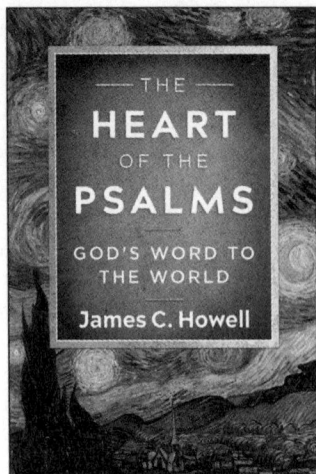